debbie tucker green

For the Royal Court: *ear for eye*; *a profoundly affectionate, passionate devotion to someone* (-noun); *hang*; *truth and reconciliation*; *random*; *stoning mary*.

Other theatre includes: *nut* (National); *generations* (Young Vic); *trade* (RSC); *born bad* (Hampstead); *dirty butterfly* (Soho).

Film and television includes: *swirl*, *second coming*, *random*.

Radio includes: *Assata Shakur: The FBI's Most Wanted Woman* (adaptation); *lament*; *gone*; *random*; *handprint*; *freefall*.

Directing includes: *a profoundly affectionate, passionate devotion to someone* (-noun); *hang*; *nut*; *truth and reconciliation* (all theatre); *second coming* (feature film); *swirl* (short film); *random* (film); *Assata Shakur: The FBI's Most Wanted Woman*; *lament*; *gone*; *random* (all radio).

Awards include: Radio Academy Arias Gold Award (*lament*); International Film Festival Rotterdam Big Screen Award (*second coming*); BAFTA for Best Single Drama (*random*); Black International Film Award for Best UK Film (*random*); OBIE Special Citation Award (*born bad*, New York Soho Rep. production); Olivier Award for Best Newcomer (*born bad*).

debbie tucker green
plays: one

born bad
dirty butterfly
generations
stoning mary
trade
random

with an Introduction by the author

NICK HERN BOOKS
London
www.nickhernbooks.co.uk

A Nick Hern Book

debbie tucker green plays: one first published in Great Britain as a paperback original in 2018 by Nick Hern Books Limited, The Glasshouse, 49a Goldhawk Road, London W12 8QP

This collection copyright © 2018 debbie tucker green
Introduction copyright © 2018 debbie tucker green

born bad copyright © 2003, 2018 debbie tucker green
dirty butterfly copyright © 2003, 2018 debbie tucker green
generations copyright © 2004 debbie tucker green
stoning mary © 2005, 2018 debbie tucker green
trade copyright © 2005, 2018 debbie tucker green
random copyright © 2008, 2018 debbie tucker green

debbie tucker green has asserted her right to be identified as the author of these works

Cover image: debbie tucker green

Designed and typeset by Nick Hern Books, London
Printed in the UK by Mimeo Ltd, Huntingdon, Cambridgeshire PE29 6XX

ISBN   978 1 84842 763 1

Contents

Introduction   vii

born bad   1

dirty butterfly   57

generations   113

stoning mary   143

trade   221

random   283

Introduction

I get asked about the dialogue, layout and punctuation of the plays. If you're finding it sticky, here are some thoughts…

'…' Before dialogue.
A character is actively thinking before speaking, it doesn't always have to relate to what they are just about to say, but the actor needs to know what that thought is and why they haven't voiced it. It may (or may not) inform how they say what follows.
However, those three dots don't need to be over-ponderous.

After dialogue '…'
This is a character trailing off in thought deciding not to carry on vocally or maybe they can't. They may be distracted by their thoughts, related or unrelated. Again though, don't linger on them for ages…

' – ' midsentence is a character's mind working faster than their mouth. It breaks their vocal flow, like they're correcting themselves or getting a quicker, better way of expressing themselves that they drop in. It's a very quick shift.

' – ' at the end of a sentence is the following character cutting off the previous person's flow with their own dialogue.

If there's no full stop between different character's lines then the following character is picking up the person's flow. Not so much cutting them off but more continuous, even if it's about something completely different or contradictory.

If a character has no dialogue and is listed above or below another character with no dialogue, there is an active silence between those listed. Can be fleeting, maybe a little longer but not long and drawn out. The actors don't have to be thinking the same thing but need to know what their own character isn't saying to the other.

If a character has an active silence on their own, that moment is for them.

A '/' is an overlapping point marking where the following character starts their dialogue.

trade does something a bit different with the '/'. It is used to break up the flow of a sentence. A bit more staccato I think.
Shit.
I wrote it ages ago. I think that's what it was.
It was.

It can all sound a bit long before you jump in, if you jump in, but it's not. Done right, the precision sounds conversational.

Anyhow. It's talking. And not talking. And how these characters do it.

dtg
2018

born bad

born bad was first performed at Hampstead Theatre, London, on 29 April 2003, with the following cast:

DAWTA   Jenny Jules
SISTER 2   Nadine Marshall
MUM   Alibe Parsons
BROTHER   Nicholas Pinnock
DAD   Ewart James Walters
SISTER 1   Sharlene Whyte

Director   Kathy Burke
Designer   Jonathan Fensom
Lighting Designer   Paul Keogan
Sound Designer   John Leonard for Aura

Characters

DAD
MUM
DAWTA
SISTER 1
SISTER 2
BROTHER

A blood-related Black family.

DAWTA *is also sister to the* SISTERS *and* BROTHER *who are also son and dawtas of* MUM *and* DAD.

Once onstage, the characters never leave.

Names appearing without dialogue indicate active silences between characters listed.

/ *denotes where dialogue starts to overlap.*

The action takes place within a day.

Preset

A solitary chair is onstage.

A female solo gospel rendition of 'What a Friend We Have in Jesus' starts through one verse...

The hymn becomes part hummed and less formed.

Fade to black.

The hymn blends, half-sung, half-hummed familiarly by MUM *(unseen) who quietly takes over the tune.*

Scene One

One chair on stage.

The hymn continues by MUM *(unseen).*

DAD *is sitting in the chair, confidently.*

DAWTA *is not.*

Silently she demands eye contact.

He finds it difficult.

DAWTA   Say it.

             Say it.

             Daddy...

             Say it.

             They make eye contact.

             She gains his lost confidence.

             The hymn draws to an end.

Scene Two

Three chairs on stage.

DAWTA *and* MUM.

DAWTA   If yu actin like a bitch

I'm a call yu it

if y'lookin like a bitch

I'm a call yu it.

If y'lookin like a bitch as you lookin on me –
I see yu and yu bitch ways – mi a go call you
it again mi noh business.

Watchin you watchin me like the bitch bitch
yu is.

I'll letcha

and I'll say it two times.

Then two times that.

Then two times that again – for yu – yu
mudda, and yu mudda's mudda – those
bitches that bred yu off before and before that
– and from before that again.

From whenever your bitch bloodline started.

From whatever bitch beginnings y'had.

Bitch.

MUM   Don't say that.

DAWTA   And I'll call it like iss nuthin, and I'll say it
like iss nuthin like the nuthin it is like the
nuthin you are like the nuthin you took a try
at to mek me.

Bitch.

Cap fit.

Bitch.

| | And I'll letcha look in my face now y'wanna – you wanna? I dunno what you wanna see, whatchu spectin on – whatchu spectin on – whatchu spectin on reflectin yu back – or is it you don't got no shadow? – But I'll letcha look – |

MUM   I'm not lookin

DAWTA   letcha mek a piece a y'eye contact –

MUM   I'm not lookin yu

DAWTA   – now. Now yu feelin – *how* yu feelin? *Now* you feelin you able – look…

            Look.

MUM   You got nothing I need to see.

            MUM *restarts humming her hymn.*

DAWTA   Look…

            Look it.

MUM   And never have had.

DAWTA   …*Watch*.

            MUM *looks at her.*

            Eh?

            Now yu ready… an now yu wanna – now y'got the bottle with y'bitch self to clock me eye to eye – woman to woman –

MUM   is what yu is?

DAWTA   Never thought I'd reach it? – Woman to woman – bitch to bitch.

            Si mi nuh.

            I'll letcha.

            Letcha look on me.

MUM   Don't call me that.

DAWTA   Wear your title wear y'crown

MUM   don't call me that

DAWTA   bitch got summink to say looks like bitch
               can't help herself, can't help herself and her
               bitch ways – can yer.

               Could yer?

               Each and every and any opportunity openin
               that twis up turn down dutty bitch mout' and
               I'm hearin nuthin but your bad bitchisms
               bouncin off your tongue – trippin off yu bitch
               breat' rippin thru to me – through y'bitch teet'
               – rippin me with your bitch prayers an 'alf a
               bitched-out hymn – rollin over to where I'm
               at, like I'm meant to hear.

               Like I wanna –

               look me –

               like I wanna hear, like I really wanna hear that
               from you.

               Again.

               Like you got summink to say.

               Now.

               Look at me. Come on.

               Like all now you got a whole heap yu gots to
               say to me lookin on me with your bitch self
               like it'd cost to look away. And I ent chargin
               yu nuthin. For nuthin. I ent chargin yu nuthin
               am I?

               See cos, I'd rather have your bitch nuthin than
               your little bit a bitch su'un – safer to have
               shittall from yu than expect and wait on a
               piece and not get a raas

MUM   you call me what I am.

DAWTA   I juss did.

MUM   Call me what I am.

DAWTA	You actin like a bitch, I'm a call you it
MUM	call me what I am.
DAWTA	You lookin like a bitch I'm a call yu it
MUM	call me what / I am
DAWTA	you sounding wholly like the holy bitch you is
MUM	or can't you?
DAWTA	Bitch you were.
MUM	Come on.
DAWTA	Bitch yu are.
MUM	Come on.
	Call me what I am.
	Call me – what I am…
	Call me Mum, then.

Scene Three

A fourth chair is added. SISTER 1.

SISTER 1	She chose.
	I remember.
DAWTA	You remember?
SISTER 1	Not *remember* remember –
DAWTA	butcha know?
SISTER 1	I recall… sorta… somethin… remember, 'alf-arsed remember like that, y'know?
DAWTA	Ask her.

SISTER 1	I'm not asking.
DAWTA	Ask her
SISTER 1	you ask her you wanna know
DAWTA	I'm not askin
SISTER 1	it's you wanna know, not me.
	You wanna know enough bad enough for long enough you'll ask – you will – you will you'll have to, so what.
DAWTA	She's a bitch.
SISTER 1	And you from her. So what?
DAWTA	And you from it an' all.
	So what does that make you –
SISTER 1	I know what I am.
DAWTA	I'm askin nothing – niche – not a raas – I got nothing / to say
SISTER 1	Butcha askin me now, you're askin me to remember – you're waiting on me to recall so yu can remember how to remember
DAWTA	*you* / know
SISTER 1	know what you wantin me to say – know you waitin on that and I've been waiting on you to ask.
	I've been waiting on you for ages.
	I've been waiting on you for years.
	And I know I wanna get it right, know you want that, I do know what you want –
DAWTA	you do remember
SISTER 1	not how you wannit I don't – I ent gonna lie – not remembering the nitty grit, not the all yu wanna know, not the whole nine, not your

	version – not all a that. I don't. But I remember bits –
DAWTA	bits ent good enough.
SISTER 1	Bits 'bout you though
DAWTA	but the bits have gotta count.
SISTER 1	Bits 'bout you do – the bits about you and some bits about her and the bit about it that it weren't me.

Come here…

She chose.

DAWTA   She chose?

SISTER 1   It wasn't by accident.

I remember that.

DAWTA   You sure y'remembrin right

SISTER 1   Sure you're still askin?

C'mere.

It wasn't by luck. It wasn't by – or lack a it. Depending.

It wasn't by misfortune. It weren't.

It weren't all your misfortune.

You weren't borned misfortunate.

More misfortunate.

Unfortunate.

Unfortunately.

Born bad. No.

Nature nurture. None a that not knowin.

Wondering long over which one.

No.

She knew.

	She chose.
DAWTA	She didn't.
SISTER 1	She chose.
DAWTA	No.
SISTER 1	She chose.
DAWTA	Cos she had to –
SISTER 1	no.
DAWTA	Cos she had to?
SISTER 1	No. She chose cos she wouldn't let him.
	I do remember that bit
DAWTA	*she* / (chose) –
SISTER 1	she picked.
	She did.
	She chose to choose she did.
	She chose you.
	Deliberate. Decisive. How she does. She did.
	Come.
DAWTA	You come here.
SISTER 1	Come.
DAWTA	You come 'ere first.
SISTER 1	S'coming back to me now –
	flooding back to me now –
DAWTA	I think I don't wanna know
SISTER 1	ent I remembering it right for yer?
DAWTA	I wouldn't know that would I?
SISTER 1	Ent I recalling it your way right?
	No?
	Cos it wasn't even close.

The choice weren't even close.

We weren't close.

The outcome weren't in the balance, me and you weren't in the balance, it weren't a drawn-out maybe me maybe you, a long lingering look at us both weren't that, we weren't never neck-and-neck tight over which one, weren't nights a sacrificin sleep over us – weren't days of deliberation she didn't deliberate for long, she never does does she?

DAWTA   You rememberin this your way / or what?

SISTER 1   I'm remembering it right.

And she made up her mind and she made her choice and she never changed it and she never has.

I swear.

Has she?

Has she?

Thank God.

And I do.

On my part.

DAWTA   God ent really figurin this side a the fence / y'know?

SISTER 1   God was who I'd give thanks to every night in gratitude, God was who I thanked for guiding her in getting her choice right or shouldn't I say –

DAWTA   no, say

SISTER 1   iss what I remember or shouldn't I say –

DAWTA

SISTER 1

DAWTA   no say.

SISTER 1   I ent gonna deny. I ent gonna play regret like I
             should like I should – should I play polite?
             We're family we're beyond – and family
             don't do polite do they? Ent got no need Sis –
             so I should wish it on me?

             Should I wish it on me?

             Or keep giving thanks that it was you?

             C'mere.

             They are close.

             Like I did.

             Pause.

DAWTA

SISTER 1

DAWTA

SISTER 1   You're strong you are.

             You got given the gift, given the gift of
             strength, you did. Give thanks for that. God
             made you like that – made you strong like that.
             Mum saw that strength, seeing that made her
             choice – made her choice easy. You made her
             choice easy, God gifting you how you are – that
             you could take it like that and I'd pray for yer.

             I remember.

             I remember that.

DAWTA   I wouldn't know.

SISTER 1   Pray for you hard

DAWTA   should I thank you?

SISTER 1   Every night with my bedtime drink in my
             bedtime pjs and my bedtime crackers and my
             bedtime prayers to your empty bed – you'd
             feature, pray to God pray to Jesus, pray to
             Mary and do Joseph up there an' all – angels
             an' ancestors. All of 'em.

DAWTA   I'm not gonna thank you

SISTER 1   and I'd pray for world peace – for Black
               power, for good grades and for Mum / and
               Dad

DAWTA   I'm not gonna thank you cos your prayers was
               / never replied

SISTER 1   for her choice, for your strength, for me not to
               have it, for our whole family and for you to
               not fail – for you to not fail – and for you to
               not fall pregnant neither.

DAWTA   Thanks for nothin.

SISTER 1   In that order.

               And my prayers got answered.

               And my prayers got answered though.

               You can't deny that.

               Can you – can't deny that.

               No one can't deny that.

               Jesus loved you Sis.

               I do remember that.

               Look how strong you are.

               Look how strong you are.

               Look at you.

               You got gifted that and I never got gifted by
               God nuthin.

DAWTA   She chose.

SISTER 1   I remember.

DAWTA   You remember.

SISTER 1   Not *remember* remember

DAWTA	but she chose?
SISTER 1	I remember that.
	I remember that.
	I do remember that it wasn't me.

Scene Four

Five chairs onstage. SISTER 2 *has joined.*

SISTER 2	Don't
	don't
	don't. Yeh.
	Don't ask –
	don't ask me
	don't ask me *nuthin*
DAWTA	I'm askin yer
SISTER 2	don't ask mi nuthin yu – mek mi feel – welcome to your worl' a darkness – mek mi feel – I don't want – don't ask me *nothin* – mek mi feel *sick* – and don't let her –
DAWTA	I'm askin
SISTER 2	don't let / her –
DAWTA	I'm / asking
SISTER 2	*don't* –
DAWTA	I am gonna ask
SISTER 2	don't mean I gotta answer.
	Or is it you gonna force me?

This is how it is.

This is how she is.

This is how it is yeh?

Sick.

How she is.

She lies. She do she does yeh. You know –
she's fuckin – she's a fuckin – yeh?

DAWTA   I'm askin

SISTER 2   move from mi – move from me wid your
               mout' and yu bad-mindedness – truss mi she's
               lyin. She is. She good at it too. She look right
               inna y'face right inna yu eye right in my face
               right there yeh – and lies like a pro –
               unflinching. Truss it. This one can lie yeh.
               Adds a smile yeh, mix it in with a nod yeh,
               stir it with a tear season it with some emotion,
               cooks it up real nice – yeh – she too lie / – she

DAWTA   You callin me a liar

SISTER 1   I don't remember –

DAWTA   I think she is.

               You callin me a liar?

SISTER 2   A low-down dutty lyin little raas claat too lie
               bitch is it and we know yeh, you know, we've
               said yeh –

SISTER 1   I don't remember the detail / – I don't –

SISTER 2   and doin it with a straight face and doin it to
               my face, yeh, blatant – that's how her lies are,
               truss mi – that's how they come, how they
               come atcha remorseless

DAWTA   you wanna know?

SISTER 2   No!

               Lissen – she manipulates – she manipulating
               – she done manipulising you, gone from you
               – and now she's trying her fuckries on me

DAWTA   you wanna know?

SISTER 2	No I don't. And don't fuck with someone who can fuck you back worse
DAWTA	exactly
SISTER 2	cos I ent playin. Ent playin yu. I ent fuckin playin with you. Look her how she works on you good – look how she thinks she worked on you good, good and subtle, good and long, good and proper so yu nah feel it good. I *know*. *I* can see – si mi y'eye dem – wide open. *Both*. Wide open to your antics – wide open to your anticatin – and it's insultin.
DAWTA	You want to know –
SISTER 2	you're insultin.

She's insultin.

You're insultin me. *And no I don't*.

She liked you. |
DAWTA	You don't even know what you don't know –
SISTER 2	know I don't wanna be like you
DAWTA	exactly.
SISTER 2	Never wanted to be like you.
DAWTA	Exactly that.
SISTER 2	And never will
DAWTA	and you should thank me / fe it
SISTER 2	*you wish*. How you love lie too much how you love drama so much how you love damage and damagin –
DAWTA	I'm damaged
SISTER 2	you ent damaged you're fucked and there's a difference. She loved you yeh – she's *upset* – Mummy's upset
DAWTA	you wanna tell her what your bedtime prayers begged for?

SISTER 2   She's upset and don't bring her to – this one
             to – to back yu

SISTER 1   I'm saying / nothing

SISTER 2   to to – reinforce for yourself – t'getcha – get
             your own back hol' dat – watch your own
             back cos she ent got it and I for sure ent.

             You made this about you, it always is about
             you and always has been from back inna the
             day. She liked you – yeh – and you know it,
             you come out first – firstborn and adored –
             yeh you was, then it was her Jesus – you was
             even ahead a him – then her, then him – then
             a next one, me – yeh, me somewhere down
             the ass end a the family tree, y'get, yeh?
             Y'get – remember

DAWTA   thass not how it was

SISTER 1   it could have been.

SISTER 2   See I ent the liar sittin here 'mongst us wolf in
             sheep's clothin yeh – lashin us with the comin-
             atcha lies am I?

             Am I?

             Cos the onliest person that fall't you from
             grace – what ever little bit you got given – was
             you. You and your own self your own-ah self –
             cah – see it, I ent the anti-man little bundle a
             bitterness sittin here lyin with whatever good
             goddamn issues you got, yeh, God knows
             why – who knows from where and who gives
             a flyin finga fuck yeh – ah noh mi – fuck dat –
             you need to move from mi – you need to
             move from mi – you need to move from me
             as well an' go weh

DAWTA   you callin me a liar?

SISTER 2   I ent call't you nuthin

DAWTA   you callin me a liar?

SISTER 2	Ent call't yu nuthin – yet – but I'll call you what I wasn't – if I want.
DAWTA	Yu to my face call me a liar – yu call me that
SISTER 2	cap fit you tell me. Liar over bitch, I dunno which. She liked you loved you. She watched you, she was careful a you
SISTER 1	she was
SISTER 2	you got her nervous of you
SISTER 1	she was.
SISTER 2	You got us all treadin on eggshells throughout over you. *She* got us all treadin on eggshells throughout over you.
	Growin up on eggshells for years yeh, thass what I recall
SISTER 1	I remember now
SISTER 2	ennit. Over you.
SISTER 1	I remember now.
SISTER 2	Ennit.
SISTER 1	The detail's comin back.
SISTER 2	Ennit.
	Yeh.
	See.
	Darin hardly to talk to yer – thass what I recall.
	Mindful a your mout' thass my recallations a years a you.
	You, moody as fuck forever – years a lookin – years a lookin on you, years a livin with, y'get?
DAWTA	She's a bitch.
SISTER 2	You are.
DAWTA	She's a bitch.

SISTER 2	You are and where you goin where you goin? Move from mi cos I know you're lyin – I know you're lyin – I was there and now you've gone and got her propah upset.
DAWTA	I'm upset
SISTER 2	you ent able.
DAWTA	I've been upset
SISTER 2	So what?
DAWTA	So my upset don't count?
SISTER 2	My point exactly, y'get?
	Beat.
	And I know you're lyin.
DAWTA	Tell her what you know.
SISTER 2	I do know you're lyin.
DAWTA	You don't know a thing
SISTER 2	and you wanna know how?
DAWTA	Yu don't know nuthin
SISTER 2	you wanna know / how?
DAWTA	And you should thank me for that
SISTER 2	you wanna know how I know?
DAWTA	I'm the liar – you tell me
SISTER 2	cos he never.
	Yeh?
	He never. Never not a once.
	Not a once – yeh.
	Never. Not my cute little head-plait wide-eye'd home-made fresh-face me, nothin.
	No'un.
	And you wantin me to look things that ent there yeh. Truss it – what? You got me lookin

things that ent there – lookin over my
shoulder when I should be lookin ahead.
Lookin him when I should be lookin you.
Wonderin 'bout things I got no business
thinkin about. That whatchu want. Yeh?

Yeh.

Thanks. Yeh. Thanks for that.

See. Not a touch, not a glance. Not a raas.
Never once.

Did he you?

SISTER 1   No.

SISTER 2   Did he you?

SISTER 1   No.

SISTER 2   See!

And you ent gonna sit there and tell me you
got summink I ent… are ya? Huh? You gonna
sit there and lie that you had a touch a
something back in the day I di'un't…

That little gurl you had something over
bouncin-baby me?

Are ya.

Like you were 'special'.

Who's gonna sit there and say that.

Who's sittin there sayin that…?

Listen…

Listen.

Beat.

Ooh. Y'know what?

Hear what – the sound a fuckin silence.

The silence a no one sayin it.

The silence a no one else sayin shit.

	You remember her 'special' like that?
SISTER 1	…No.
SISTER 2	You remember her special like that?
SISTER 1	No.
SISTER 2	See.

Nobody.

So you wanna keep your anti-man, anti-fam, lyin sentiment to yourself yeh cos I had a great time – I had a fuckin great time – yeh I did – great time growin up – didn't we

SISTER 1   I –

SISTER 2   didn't we

SISTER 1   I don't / remember

SISTER 2   truss me.

SISTER 1   I don't remember

SISTER 2   you will – and I couldn't a asked for a better piece a parentin yeh and a lovelier start to life and the all that it should be the all that it should be me havin a fuckin ball yeh – havin the time a my fuckin little life in my start-up years – the ones that matter – yeh – truss mi – the ones you remember – the fuckin formative ones that stay with y'get, the ones that stick, the ones that is most important y'know? And the only problem bein – the only issue, the only fucked-up piece a fam business memoryin me – carryin on messin with the programme from back in the day –

yeh…

was *you*.

That's how it was.

So don't step to me don't step to mi – don't step to me and ask me *nuthin* – don'tchu dare.

Scene Five

Five chairs onstage. DAD *and* SISTER 2.

They sit.

SISTER 2 *smiles at her* DAD.

SISTER 2   Say it Daddy.

                 Say it.

Scene Six

Six chairs onstage. DAWTA *and* BROTHER.

BROTHER   You never did didja.

DAWTA

BROTHER

DAWTA

BROTHER   You never did.

                 Beat.

                 You never knew

DAWTA   he said I was the only one.

BROTHER   You never knew the half you didn't.

DAWTA   Thought I was the only one didn't I.

BROTHER   Didn't know jack – don't know dick –
                 demandin to know now and you don't even
                 know what the question is.

                 Beat.

DAWTA   All the things she wouldn't do.

BROTHER   No, all the things she couldn't do.

DAWTA   Said she wouldn't do anythin…

BROTHER   She couldn't do what I did.

DAWTA   Said she'd never do nuthin

BROTHER   she wouldn't do what I did

DAWTA   that she wouldn't even try.

             Why wouldn't she try.

             Why wouldn't she try?

             Did she know she wouldn't like it?

             D'you think she wouldn't like it?

BROTHER   Did you?

DAWTA   Did you?

BROTHER   Didja try to?

DAWTA   So – did you then?

             Beat.

BROTHER   (*Dry.*) All the things you wouldn't do I guess,
             I got. All your little –

DAWTA   there was nothing I wouldn't do.

             Brother.

             There was no choice.

             So.

             Beat.

             So whichever way he twis yu out whatever
             way he done you… is whatever way he
             wanted, I guess.

             Or whatever you let him.

             Pause.

BROTHER   Heard you cussed her out

DAWTA   we had words.

BROTHER   Heard you bitched her right out

DAWTA   we had a moment y'know.

BROTHER	Heard she's upset
DAWTA	a mother-dawta piece a quality time.
BROTHER	Wish I'd been there
DAWTA	been there for me right?
BROTHER	Been there to hear your mout' – so.
DAWTA	Been there for me, right?
BROTHER	Been there to hear that.
	She's upset
DAWTA	good.
BROTHER	Really upset.
DAWTA	Gooder.
BROTHER	You really done her.

Beat.

DAWTA	There you go.

Beat.

BROTHER	He chose me.
DAWTA	
BROTHER	
DAWTA	
BROTHER	He chose me y'know and she didn't have a clue – so.
DAWTA	…I wished you'd been there – and I love you to bits –
BROTHER	she don't know nothin.
DAWTA	I love ya t'bits but you ent remembrin right
BROTHER	…he told me I was the only –
DAWTA	so he said the same shit to me, said the same shit to me.
	She said the same shit to me

BROTHER   and now you're tellin me I weren't and that
           I'm remembrin all wrong

DAWTA   yeh –

BROTHER   that I'm not

DAWTA   yeh –

BROTHER   that you were his only one an' all

DAWTA   well. Yeh.

BROTHER   Which makes me what – which makes me
           what? Which makes me more nuthin then

DAWTA   well – no.

BROTHER   Don't mek mi somethin –

DAWTA

BROTHER   Don't make me special.

DAWTA   We never was.

BROTHER   Don't mek mi yu.

DAWTA   No.

BROTHER   Don't mek mi what I thought I was –

DAWTA   which was –

BROTHER   what he told me I was

DAWTA   – no.

BROTHER   Don't mek mi that.

DAWTA   Don't mek mi that neither – so.

           DAWTA *goes to give him a touch.*

BROTHER   Whass that gonna do.

           Whass that gonna do?

           Don't.

DAWTA   …Really?

BROTHER   Really, don't.

DAWTA   Really?

BROTHER   Really… cos.

            Beat.

            Cos… just.

            Beat.

DAWTA   I'm askin.

BROTHER

DAWTA

BROTHER   What am I sposed to do with that?

            Whatchu wantin me to do with that?

            Whatchu askin me for?

            Whatchu tellin me for?

            Whatchu tellin me for now?

DAWTA

BROTHER

DAWTA   So. She knew.

            BROTHER *shakes his head.*

BROTHER   No.

            And she won't.

DAWTA

BROTHER   I ent got nuthin to say about that, ent got
            nuthin to say to you 'bout that attall… you
            gonna gimme a squeeze to mek it go away, I
            got jack to say – got shittall to give yer I got
            fuckall to say – I didn't bring this up and I
            wouldn'ta – I wouldn'ta

DAWTA   so don't say nuthin then.

BROTHER   I wouldn'ta – not like / that.

DAWTA   So say / nothin.

BROTHER   'Cept yu shu'unt a call't her what / you did –

DAWTA   Maybe I di'unt call her / that –

BROTHER	call him a liar yes – but don't call her what you did.
DAWTA	I didn't.
BROTHER	She's our mum she borned us out and I ent sayin shit. I ent sayin niche.
DAWTA	…She tell you I called her that?
	I didn't.
	Beat.
BROTHER	I'm sayin fuckall.
	Beat.
DAWTA	…If I'd (said) –
BROTHER	buthcu di'unt.
DAWTA	But if I'd / said –
BROTHER	Butcha never.
DAWTA	But –
BROTHER	'but'
DAWTA	but –
BROTHER	but you never said nuthin all now – so now we'll never know what coulda cos you di'unt say dick didja?
DAWTA	Neither did you
BROTHER	neither did you
DAWTA	neither did you
BROTHER	not to you I never done, no…
	Beat.
DAWTA	…What?
BROTHER	
DAWTA	
BROTHER	

DAWTA	…Well…
	Beat.
	To who then…?
	Beat.
	What?
	What.
	Pause.
	(*To* SISTER 1.) Eh?…Yo…
	…Yo…
	Yeow! You –
SISTER 1	you never asked me to remember that bit.
	Beat.
	You never asked me to remember that.
DAWTA	Pray for him an' all didja?
SISTER 1	Hard.
DAWTA	Harder'n me?
SISTER 1	Hard as.
DAWTA	Every night like me?
SISTER 1	…Almost.
DAWTA	Sounds like you spent most a your years on the down-low prayin to the most high you did
SISTER 1	what, while you was just spendin yours – on the down-low – weren't it.
DAWTA	You tell me.
SISTER 1	You did.
DAWTA	…Real revelation your selective remembrin's turnin out to be, really somethin.
	How long you known?
SISTER 1	I can't remember.
DAWTA	When did he say?

SISTER 1   How 'bout I can't recall that / neither

DAWTA   Wanna hand to help do yer? Y'wanna hand to
t'knock some remembrin into yer

SISTER 1   you wanna watch yourself –

DAWTA   and yu wanna watch your mouth.

SISTER 1   Sorry – wash my mouth?

DAWTA   Wanna *watch* your mouth

SISTER 1   *wash it?*

DAWTA   You heard.

SISTER 1   Thought you were doin a Dad then. Or what I
remember you doin after you'd done doin –

BROTHER   I told her not to say nothin and I told her back
in the day and she didn't say and so it's down
to me –

SISTER 1   I do remember that bit. Hearing you – me
hearing that.

Thinkin you had the cleanest teeth in the
world…

DAWTA

SISTER 1

DAWTA   Help him through it didja?

SISTER 1   Yes.

DAWTA   Yeh?

BROTHER   Yes.

DAWTA   Is it.

Beat.

SISTER 1   …You never asked…

DAWTA   Didn't know there was queue did I.

Beat.

SISTER 1   You never asked

DAWTA   so I didn't get. You just said.

SISTER 1   …You never asked for nothing.

DAWTA

SISTER 1   Never nuthin.

                Never disciplined for bein late down you was.
                Breakfast.

                Even on a schoolday…

                And you never wondered why he weren't
                down the mornings you was?

                And it was me who'd pack your school bag
                knowin you wouldn't have time…

                And it was me laid out your school clothes
                knowin you wouldn't have time…

                And it was me who weren't allowed to get
                down from table, let alone out before she'd
                give the say-so.

                You didn't even have to be there.

DAWTA   *Now* you wanna swap?

SISTER 1   No.

                No I wouldn't.

                And you never wondered why he weren't
                down there the mornings you was?

                There wasn't a science to it.

                Beat.

BROTHER   It's really not rocket science.

DAWTA   …Why didn't you say?

BROTHER   I –

SISTER 1   he doesn't like that.

DAWTA   And you know.

SISTER 1	He doesn't like being touched like that.
DAWTA	You know?
BROTHER	She does.
DAWTA	She does?
	Does she?!
	Oh.
BROTHER	
DAWTA	
BROTHER	
SISTER 1	It's not always all about you, y'know –
DAWTA	he said it was only me (*To* SISTER 1.) and I didn't wannit to be you, (*To* BROTHER.) and I blieved him, brother.
	So.
BROTHER	Got me blievin it was only me though
DAWTA	and he chose you, so that makes you somethin.
	She picked me.
BROTHER	He said it was all the things she cu'unt do
DAWTA	nah, said it was all the things she wouldn't do, so.
	Said she never did nuthin – so.
BROTHER	So he chose me.
DAWTA	See.
	So tell me, why, why didn't she even try?

Scene Seven

SISTER 1	No.
SISTER 2	You?
BROTHER	…No.
DAWTA	Deny deny deny, y'gonna do mi like Chris's last day you are
SISTER 2	and definitely not me.
	See. So.
BROTHER	I don't believe
DAWTA	you're a Judas.
BROTHER	…I'm a non-believer.
DAWTA	You can tell.
BROTHER	Blieve in the devil though.
SISTER 2	See 'ar deh.
DAWTA	
SISTER 1	Ask her
DAWTA	I'm not askin
SISTER 2	you ask her seein as you love distress and destruction and the day ent even done yet – hear what – y'still got time to piss more of us off y'know. You still got nuff time and yu still don'ts give-a-shit so why yu don't tek yu'self an ask her and top your talent a today's tormentation.
BROTHER	I'm not sayin nuthin
DAWTA	surprise surprise.
BROTHER	Just like you did.

DAWTA	Don't.
SISTER 1	Ask her, stop your sufferation.
SISTER 2	Stop ours.
BROTHER	I'm not askin.
DAWTA	I'm not askin
BROTHER	I'm not sayin nuthin.
DAWTA	I'm not gonna ask her neither.
SISTER 1	How bad do you wanna know then?
SISTER 2	Joker.
	Beat.
SISTER 1	Ask her
SISTER 2	stop our sufferating.
	Stop our sufferating you.
	Ask her.
	Ask her.
	Stop you askin us. *Sis.*
	Ask her.
	Go on.
DAWTA	Firstborn over second…
	Boy over gurl.
	Husban' over wifey…
	Beat.
	Wifey over child…
	Sista over brotha.
	Mother over dawta.
	Liar over bitch
MUM	you tell me.
DAWTA	No you tell me Mum, you tell me.

And you should know that I know. That she
told me so that I would. And – what she *said*
– well…

MUM   Well?

DAWTA   Well. You know what I know I know you do.

And I'm wonderin to and after to and feelin to
know y'know just how easy – she said it was
easy… That you found it easy, that you had
no doubts hardly hesitate and I dunno xactly
what she remembers whether she's
remembrin right whether she's rememberin it
all but she said you done what you did – you
chose what you did – she says she remembers
that.

MUM   Well –

DAWTA   and if that was your choice how come I had to
figure – if that was the choice how come I had
to feature at all? How come you never chose
to leave me outta it like you did them? How
come I couldn'ta not known about it like she
did and had the glorious growin-up years like
this one?

How come you never chose for me to do that.

How come that then?

How come you did me like that?

How come you played me like wifey when I
shoulda stayed playin dawta? Cos dawta was
what I was.

What I am and I weren't you. I shouldn'ta
been doin what you shoulda done – what you
wouldn'ta done was it? And you shouldn'ta
chose me to.

MUM   Well.

She's remembering wrong.

DAWTA   She remembers that bit.

MUM   She's remembering wrong

DAWTA   she remembers, Mum. She remembers you
                  Mum.

                  She remembers you on your knees to Jesus
                  prayin I'd be on my knees to him – that you'd
                  be on your knees to Jesus prayin I'd stay on my
                  knees in your place and y'can't deny the power
                  a prayer can yer, can't say they never got heard,
                  you can't deny God giftin you that, can yer?

                  God gifted you somethin.

                  She remembers that. Mum.

                  She got that bit right.

                  Cos I was on my knees longer lost for longer
                  in position longer than the longest a your
                  pitiful prayers could be.

                  And you know.

MUM   Do I.

DAWTA   You know

MUM   I remember

DAWTA   so did she.

MUM   I remember.

DAWTA   Yeh she did

MUM   I remember what you were like.

                  Look.

DAWTA   What I was – what I was made to be like.

MUM   Look at me.

                  I remember that exactly.

                  That. I do.

                  So.

                  From the out I knew. I knew you was born
                  bad right from the beginning –

DAWTA   so what y'did born me out for?

So why yu did born me out for?

Beat.

MUM   Why do you think?

Beat.

…Still can't look at me?

So…

How yu were.

How you were, how yu were mekkin you how you are.

How y'were with me how yu was in the house how yu were with him from birth.

So.

Your truth don't taste to me. Your memory don't really matter – you carry on as sour as you want as sour as you did as much as you are.

DAWTA   Mum –

MUM   you put me on my knees you did, you put me on my knees prayin for survival and kept me there and you put yourself on your knees or what ever else you ended up on, all by yourself.

DAWTA   Mum –

MUM   all by your ownsome. Wid no help from we.

Looking…? Still?

And here…

There was nothing for me to choose that you hadn't chosen for yourself was there and you won't remember that and you won't recall going boutcha business like you grown like that.

Look at me when I'm talkin t'you.

Won't remember beggin to be big before you was like that – wishin you a woman before graduating from bein a girl like that and couldn't handle what you had – you won't remember that will you won't go memory *that* and there was a bitch in a the house – yes

DAWTA	she said, you chose me
MUM	*look at me.* There was a bitch in the place yes –
DAWTA	said you chose me over her
MUM	there was a bitch under the roof yes – but you should know that the bitch of the family wasn't me.

So.

Beat.

So if I did mek a choice.

You made it easy.

Scene Eight

BROTHER *and* DAD.

Pause.

BROTHER	You gonna say sumthin…
	Pause.
DAD	I don't have to, Son.
	BROTHER *is close to tears.*

Scene Nine

BROTHER	What's your problem?
SISTER 2	I don't / have a
BROTHER	What is your problem?
SISTER 2	I don't got a problem *thank you*
BROTHER	I think you have
SISTER 2	which is the problem / you've got –
BROTHER	you're / not
SISTER 2	the problem you've got
BROTHER	you're not / my
SISTER 2	the problem you've got with me.
BROTHER	You're not my problem you're not – you're thing is is that you got issues.
SISTER 2	I've not / got
BROTHER	You've / got
SISTER 2	I ent / got
BROTHER	inside here –
SISTER 2	I've not got no issues. *Thank you*.
BROTHER	Buried deep-down dark / ones
SISTER 2	Thank you but –
BROTHER	buried deep-down inside here that's what you've got – what you / have
SISTER 2	thank you – yeh. But. No. Bro.
BROTHER	Drama –
SISTER 2	uh?
BROTHER	Drama.

SISTER 2	Is it.
BROTHER	Drama and denials and
SISTER 2	pure Mary J is it?
BROTHER	You tell me
SISTER 2	no. You're telling me. And what you're wishin on me is sayin a whole heap about you, brother, sayin a whole heap – ringing out loud and clear that you spending too much time inna 'ar company – she gots you well covered, well and converted well and corruption well and convinced cos you startin to sound like her and her can't stand nobody who ain't – and she sounds like she can't tek me just bein, just bein – an yu suspiciously soundin the same
BROTHER	just being a happy heap a you.
SISTER 2	So fuck her – yes – juss a ecstatic buncha bein me in here, yeh.
DAWTA	You are as vacuous as that.
BROTHER	Juss the all it is a bein you
SISTER 2	you have no idea how good that is. An' now alla a sudden iss a problem and she gone green y'eye.
DAWTA	You are as conceit' as that.
SISTER 2	And I ent carryin your cross or her'n to bring my shit down to her level
BROTHER	to bring your happy shit down to her level
SISTER 2	to bring my happy, 'static, easy-goin shit down to her ground zero – no.
DAWTA	You wouldn't. And I wouldn't ask.
SISTER 2	You couldn't ask me nuthin and I am ignorin yer –
DAWTA	you wouldn't know where / to start.

SISTER 2   I am ignorin yer.

DAWTA   You wouldn't have a clue

SISTER 2   I can't hear yer is how thorough my ignorin
yer is – y'get?

DAWTA   Still waitin for you to thank me.

SISTER 2   Ignored.

DAWTA   And you know it.

SISTER 2   *Ignored*.

DAWTA   You *know* it.

SISTER 2   I can't hear yer – I can't hear yer. I *can't*…

and t'ank yu fe what?

DAWTA   Why'dya think?

BROTHER   Why do you think?

Beat.

DAWTA   Think about it.

SISTER 2   …

DAWTA   I know.

I would know.

Beat.

SISTER 2   You're not mekkin me come inna your misery
like how you got him.

You're not getting me drag down to your
depths like how y'pullin on him.

You're not getting me goin there for your
sport.

I won't.

I'm happy for you to not be here yeh.

More'n happy for you not to be near, yeh,
y'get?

I like it when you ent and it ent hard.

It ent hard.

Yu ent hard to not like.

And see it, if you happy carryin on ignorant.

I'm happy keepin on ignorin yer.

It's easy for me keepin on ignorin yer.

Easy.

And me and he is havin a convo – an 'A', 'B' chat.

An 'A' an 'B' chat that 'C' weren't invited in on – so you need to –

DAWTA   he don't like bein touched.

SISTER 2   Huh?

DAWTA   He don't like bein touched like that.

SISTER 2   What – you tellin me how I can deal wid him all now?

That mi c'yant give Brodda a squeeze all now?

Yu exclusivisin him like that is it? Now yu gots the audacities to be tellin / me that?

DAWTA   I'm tellin you he don't like it

SISTER 2   you getting confuse you is, you getting confuse cos it's you no one don't wants to skin to skin.

DAWTA   Ask him.

SISTER 2   Fuck off.

DAWTA   Ask him.

SISTER 2   Fuck. Off.

BROTHER   Ask me.

SISTER 2   Do yer…?

Beat.

See.

BROTHER	No.
SISTER 2	
BROTHER	
SISTER 2	Why you lettin her drag you down into her misery?
	Why yu lettin y'self down lettin her drag you into her home-made misery a that? Is what she wants lookin company there, yeh.
	Why yu lettin her do that when what she wants is for one piece a misery to become two?
BROTHER	Maybe she lifts me outta mine.
SISTER 2	Your misery bein exactly what?
BROTHER	I know she lifts me outta mine.
SISTER 2	Your misery bein xactly what... then?
BROTHER	
SISTER 2	
DAWTA	
SISTER 2	
SISTER 2	... Well – you there both be miserable together then, cos alla sudden she raised in a fam I don't recognise, she's raised in a fam I don't got no recollection of and you joinin her, alla a sudden iss like I ent been involved in the last twenty –
BROTHER	you recognise it?
SISTER 1	I don't remember
SISTER 2	leave her, she confusing herself.
BROTHER	You recognise it?
SISTER 1	Bits
SISTER 2	bits don't count. Bits ents good enough.

DAWTA	Depends on what the / bits are –
SISTER 2	*You're ignored* and the bits don't make the bulk and the bulk don't mek the whole and the all a your bits together don't make your versions true and never will.
BROTHER	You sure about what you're sure about.
SISTER 2	I'm sure about that.
BROTHER	You're sure about what you're sure about are yer?
SISTER 2	Thass my 'issue'. Thass 'my problem', y'get.
BROTHER	And that's her point.
SISTER 2	And I'm well sure about her.
	Well sure about her.
	I'm sure about Mum, cos she's well upset.
	I'm sure about this one, though she's playin like she ent sure about sheself.
	I'm sure about him cos he's just... Dad.
	And –
BROTHER	you sure about me?
SISTER 2	I'm sure aboutcha.
BROTHER	Are yer?
SISTER 2	I'm sure aboutcha, yeh...
	I am.
	I'm sure that...
	I'm sure that...
	Beat.
BROTHER	You wouldn't know where to start cos you don't know shit for sure you don't, and you know it.
	You know it.
	Thass you.

	That's her point.
	And that's your –
SISTER 2	I don't / have a
BROTHER	that is your problem.
SISTER 2	I don't have problem which is the problem you've / got –
BROTHER	You're not / my
SISTER 2	the problem you've got with me.
BROTHER	You're not my problem you're not.
	Believe.
	Your thing is that you got issues
SISTER 2	I've not / got –
BROTHER	inside here.
SISTER 2	…I've not got no issues.
BROTHER	Deep-down dark ones inside there that's what you've got you have…
	Pause.
SISTER 2	…Thank you. Yeh.
	But.
	No.
	Bro.

Scene Ten

DAWTA *and* BROTHER.

Pause.

DAWTA

DAWTA

DAWTA

BROTHER

DAWTA

           Beat.

BROTHER   Worth it?

DAWTA

BROTHER

BROTHER   Worth it?

           Beat.

           Is it worth all this?

Scene Eleven

Five chairs on stage.

All are seated except DAWTA, *who wants to be.*

SISTER 1 *is sitting next to* DAD.

SISTER 2 *sits the other side of him.*

DAWTA   (And) don't mind me.

           Don't mind me

SISTER 2   what we been tryin, y'get?

DAWTA   Don't mind me.

SISTER 2   That's the point.

MUM   Yu young

DAWTA   *she's* younger.

MUM   And?

SISTER 2   And.

DAWTA   And.

SISTER 2   And far as I'm concerned –

DAWTA	butcha ent are ya?
SISTER 2	As far as I'm concerned
DAWTA	concern don't carry with / you
SISTER 2	but can I speak though – or is this still all about you?
MUM	Again.
SISTER 1	This reminds me a many a mornin back in the day.
SISTER 2	Breakfast.
MUM	'Cept you ent late down on this occasion…
SISTER 2	Huh?
BROTHER	I ent movin.
SISTER 2	Neither am I.
DAWTA	Did I stutter? I never asked.
SISTER 1	Can sit here if you want
SISTER 2	there you go.
DAWTA	No thanks.
SISTER 1	Can sit here.
MUM	There yu are.
SISTER 2	There you go.
DAWTA	What, guilt givin yu the get-up? No thanks.
SISTER 1	My conscience is clear
DAWTA	little bit you got
SISTER 2	which is a whole heap more'n you have see, so you ent serious 'bout sittin then are yer turnin down the only offer y'got so stan' there – steh there an sshh.

Listen.

…Listen.

Beat.

	Ooh! The sound a no one offerin.

SISTER 2 *laughs*.

SISTER 1 *gets up*.

DAWTA	I don't wannit.
SISTER 1	Here.
DAWTA	I don't wannit don't bother bother on my account.
SISTER 1	Here.
DAWTA	I'm fine.
SISTER 1	I'm fine too
DAWTA	not as fine as. Never as fine as.
SISTER 1	I've done with my sittin. So.
DAWTA	You sure.
	You sure about that?
	I'm *fine*
BROTHER	are yer.
MUM	Sit.

Beat.

DAWTA	Y'know what, all of a sudden – all now – I feel good to stand, somehow sittin ent doin it for me any more. I'm gonna stand here. I'm gonna go stand just here –
MUM	sit down
DAWTA	just here. Right over here.
MUM	Sit.
DAWTA	See. That's how alright I am.
SISTER 2	Hear that Mum, hear what – she's alright, she's okay. She's okay, but how 'bout you? How you doin? Anybody askin.
	Anyone wanna know?

BROTHER	Behave.
DAWTA	Listen.
	Listen.
	Beat.
	Ooh.
	Hear what?
	The sound a friggin silence – I don't think we do.
SISTER 2	Is it?
BROTHER	Behave you.
	Here.
	I'll sit there.
DAWTA	You stay where you are
BROTHER	I'll move there you sit here –
DAWTA	I ent tellin you to move –
BROTHER	you couldn't 'tell' me anything.
DAWTA	I ent askin you to move there.
BROTHER	Y'couldn't ask me nuthin.
DAWTA	
BROTHER	
DAWTA	
BROTHER	It's an offer.
DAWTA	You wanna?
BROTHER	I will.

BROTHER *crosses and sits in the vacant chair next to* DAD. *It is difficult for him.*

DAWTA *goes to move to* BROTHER*'s vacant seat but* SISTER 2 *switches place and quickly sits in his.*

The only vacant seat is another next to DAD.

Beat.

SISTER 2   …What?

DAWTA   Yu been born a bitch or what?

SISTER 2   That mek two a we then and that's two of us
you cussed out, moved on from Mum have
yer and it's three of us now that's moved and
you still ent happy see, so I sugges' thass
sayin somethin 'bout *you one*.

DAWTA   …

Beat.

SISTER 2   Iss a free country still and there's a space goin
over there, so –

MUM   *sit down*.

SISTER 1   Who?

SISTER 2   Well Mummy ent talkin to me.

DAWTA   Well I ent

SISTER 2   and his arse is seated.

DAWTA   I ent gonna

SISTER 2   so that leaves –

SISTER 1   and I don't wanna.

DAWTA   Liar.

SISTER 2   Iss a chair.

SISTER 1   It is.

SISTER 2   Iss a / chair –

DAWTA   (*Dry*.) Never.

SISTER 2   Iss a chair – not a problem. Not a problem,
not a issue – no drama – it's a

SISTER 1   chair.

DAWTA   So sit inna it then.

MUM	A seat.
SISTER 2	A chair
DAD	a chair. Sit down.
SISTER 2	See it. Juss that.
	A friggin piece a fuckrie furniture – sorry Mum – Dad –
	but it is.
	See, so if we can – you can.
	If he can – even him – him one cyan – how come you can't – siddown. What?
	Sit down – what!
SISTER 1	It is just a
DAWTA	don't.
SISTER 1	It is only a
DAWTA	please. Ah beg.
	Don't.
SISTER 2	He can.
	He can.
	How come you can't?
DAWTA	Ask him.
SISTER 2	How come that then?
DAWTA	Ask him
SISTER 2	how come that – how come that then? – See something about this ent righted – somewhere somethin ent runnin true this piece just don't add up – he will – you won't?
DAWTA	He ent me.
SISTER 2	He will. You / won't.
DAWTA	And yu ent asked him yet.
SISTER 2	…How come then…

	How is it that then, Bro...?
	Beat.
DAWTA	Don't.
BROTHER	It is –
DAWTA	don't, y'know
BROTHER	...only –
DAWTA	don't do this –
BROTHER	a chair.
	Beat.
MUM	And why wouldn't he?
BROTHER	Listen
DAWTA	don't.
SISTER 2	So, how does that work then?
MUM	Why wouldn't he?
BROTHER	Listen –
SISTER 1	just sit down, just sit there just –
MUM	why would he not want to –
SISTER 1	*just sit.*
SISTER 2	Why don't you tek the weight off...?
SISTER 1	It don't matter just do it –
SISTER 2	tek the weight off –
MUM	why would it matter to him –
DAWTA	ask your son.
BROTHER	*Lissen –*
SISTER 2	sit down before yu drop down, why don'tcha?
SISTER 1	juss kotch up. Kotch up. Perch. Please. Just sit down.
MUM	Why would it matter to him?
DAWTA	Ask your son.

BROTHER	Listen, I'm sayin –
SISTER 1	*sit.*
SISTER 2	Sit.
MUM	Ask him what?
DAD	Sit down.
SISTER 1	…Sit down…
MUM	Ask him why?
DAD	Do it.
SISTER 2	Sit, man.
	It's a chair.
BROTHER	…Do it…
	Beat.
DAD	Do it.
	Beat.
	Do it.
	Pause.
MUM	Ask our son what?

Scene Twelve

Five chairs as before.

All are seated as Scene Eleven.

DAWTA is seated on the floor between DAD's legs.

The fifth chair is empty.

DAWTA is quietly half-singing, half-humming the hymn 'What a Friend We Have in Jesus'.

SISTER 2 is close to tears.

The hymn, half-sung/hummed, bleeds into the following scene.

Scene Thirteen

MUM *cries oddly, silently. Awkward. It's been a while.*

BROTHER *carelessly offers her a hanky.*

BROTHER   So.

                 Now you know.

                 MUM *wipes her nose, but lets her eyes run freely.*

                 She offers him the hanky back.

                 Keep it.

                 The humming of the hymn stops.

Scene Fourteen

DAD *and* MUM.

Silence.

MUM

MUM

MUM

DAD

MUM

MUM   Say it…

                 Beat.

                 Say it…

                 …Say something then.

                 Pause.

...It doan matter what...

Pause.

DAD   You made the wrong choice.

End.

dirty butterfly

for Dona Daley
peace

thanks to the royal court, ruth little, caryl and my spars

dirty butterfly was first performed at Soho Theatre, London, on 26 February 2003, with the following cast:

AMELIA	Sharon Duncan-Brewster
JO	Jo McInnes
JASON	Mark Theodore

Director	Rufus Norris
Designer	Katrina Lindsay
Lighting Designer	Nigel Edwards
Sound Designer	Paul Arditti

Characters

AMELIA, *Black*
JASON, *Black*
JO, *Black or white*

Act One: the characters are always onstage, their dialogue is always to each other (if not all the characters at the same time) and never to the audience.

/ denotes where dialogue starts to overlap.

Music track (if used): 'Secret Place' by Jhelisa (from 12-inch, not album version).

JO, JASON *and* AMELIA *onstage.*

JO	I am sorry. I am sorry… I'm sorry… sorry et cetera.
	AMELIA *sings, increasing her volume to try to drown out the repetitive sound of* JO.
JASON	Sssh.
	Beat.
JO	You ever?
JASON	(*To* AMELIA.) You ever –
AMELIA	(*To* JASON.) You ever got that feelin –
JO	you ever –
AMELIA	got that restless kinda feelin.
JASON	You ever –
AMELIA	got that can't find somethin to match your mood kinda feelin – you ever got that, Jase?
JO	You ever –
JASON	found yourself doin somethin you can't help.
AMELIA	You ever / got –
JASON	Gotcha self doin somethin you can't stop?
	Beat.
	'Melia?
AMELIA	No.
JO	You ever woken up of a mornin wonderin this was gonna be your last? You ever got that feelin in your stomach as you lay there wonderin?
JASON	You ever found yourself feelin that?
AMELIA	No.

JO   Like butterflies.
                Like butterflies gone ballistic.
                Butterflies gone wrong.

JASON   You ever –

AMELIA   no once. Take it twice. *Nah*. I haven't.

JO   Woke up this mornin like that I did, and lay
                there lookin across at him.

JASON   In my room I sit there listenin out for him 'n'
                all.
                Me by myself – listening out. Hard for him –
                hard for her –

AMELIA   you're getting worse you are

JO   me looking up above us, laying there in our
                duvet over us – looking across at husband and
                wondering if this morning was gonna be my
                last.

AMELIA   You're getting worse you are.

JASON   And you're not?
                Like you're normal.

AMELIA   Like you're a role model for it is it? You the
                logo for normality is it?

JO   Have a touch a mine.

AMELIA   You the name brand – I'm just the Primark, is
                it?

JO   Take a touch a mine.

AMELIA   Don't think so somehow.
                See – how 'bout she lettin me get back to the
                normal that I know.
                The mornins that I knew.

JO

AMELIA   How 'bout that then?
                How 'bout her mornins not infringin on
                mine?

JO   It gets worse.

JASON	how 'bout her mornins not infringin on mine?
AMELIA	Xactly.
JO	It got worse.
AMELIA	Jase –
JASON	ssshh.
AMELIA	You are getting worse. You really are.
JASON	How 'bout you not sleepin on your sofa?
AMELIA	How 'bout you makin it to your bed?
JASON	How 'bout you makin it up your stairs –
AMELIA	how 'bout that then Jay?
JASON	You ever / tried doin what I –
AMELIA	My sofa ent no sofa bed. And my downstairs ent no bedroom. But I can sleep on it –
JO	is it?
AMELIA	Sleep in it –
JO	(*Amused*.) is it?
AMELIA	Got used to it good.
JO	Ent you got a perfectly good bedroom up your stairs though? Now, I'm sure you got a perfectly good bedroom / up your stairs…
AMELIA	And I wash in my downstairs sink –
JASON	you don't have to
AMELIA	do my teeth in there an' all.
JASON	You don't have to.
AMELIA	And you don't have to sit up there, be up there, Jason. It's not compulsory.
JASON	Unlike the art a sleepin in your front room.
AMELIA JASON	

JO	Knew today had potential. Knew that today was gonna kick. Me it. Or it me. Knew from the reluctant-wakin, eye-glue poppin, dead-leg stretchin of the meetin of the morning, that today – was gonna kick. And I was up for it. I was, was just… really / up for it.
AMELIA	Up that mornin – up *that* early – and before I'm out Jase – before I *deliberately leave* to go out – I'm just in my yard – in my front room – on my sofa – lookin me somethin. DJ to do me a favour and play me somethin nice on the fm, on the downstairs radio – a 'don't-mind-what', y'know. A 'don't-mind- me', y'know – somethin hollow from the radio –
JO	you can singalong to. Great.
AMELIA	…Even before I'm up to wash. I'm just lookin me a – and my upstairs radio's left on in the bathroom, talkin. And my only telly's upstairs in the empty bedroom – on. But down here my batteries are dead –
JASON	I'm not lookin anything.
JO	Don't use his eyes much does he?
AMELIA	My batteries died a death. Leavin me listenin to niche and my CDs idle.
JASON	I'm busy listening
JO	he always will
JASON	she givin me summink to lissen to for free.
JO	I give the people what they want….
AMELIA	My CDs is idle – and I don't do silents – is it. So. Me tryin t'summon up su'un to sing – a tune that comes out nice, nice to make me feel lovely – lovely makin me feel special,

	specially me knowin that I'm not. Aye Jase?
	Am I Jase?…
	Am I Jason?
	How 'bout that then? That's all I'm lookin. I was lookin a tune, Jason.
JASON	I know.
AMELIA	This is my mornin.
JASON	I know.
AMELIA	And know that I'm down here not going up. Inna mi own yard. Not goin up. How 'bout – not goin up. Not goin up. Not goin up.
JO	You said
AMELIA	I'm not goin up to hear –
JASON	Her.
AMELIA	*She*.
JO	I know.
AMELIA	Bleedin thru.
JO	I know.
AMELIA	A tune.
JASON	I know.
AMELIA	So I won't feel bad.
JASON	Then don't.
AMELIA	Don't feel bad.
JO	You won't.
AMELIA	Cos that's all I was doin.
JO	You said.
JASON	Tell her she's disturbing you.

AMELIA	I can hear y'know.
JASON	Tell her to leave you alone.
JO	Tell me then.
JASON	Tell her you can hear her.
AMELIA	Leave me alone.
	JO *is amused.*
JASON	Tell her you can't sleep in your upstairs no more –
JO	c'mon then.
JASON	Tell her how she –
JO	I dare ya –
JASON	tell her –
JO	double dare ya –
JASON	tell her –
JO	*tell me then.*
AMELIA	I can't stand the waking up to hearing you any more. I can't stand you. I can't stand the you and your him nex door to me. You and your bad – both a yers nex door to me – you and your bad – sex – nex to me – nex door to me, nex door to my bedroom. I can't stand the bad a that, any more.
JO	Bad sex over bein bad-minded.
AMELIA	Bad-minded over havin bad taste.
JO	Bad taste over havin bad music –
AMELIA	there ent nuthin wrong with my music. There ent nuthin wrong with my / music –
JO	Y'music or y'voice?
AMELIA	Don't be tryinta dis my vocalality –
JO	skills.

AMELIA	You ever / try and cuss my –
JO	(*Mocking*.) *You ever* / is it?
AMELIA	Fuck off Jo.
JO	…No.
	Beat.
AMELIA	And I walk to work.
JO	And.
AMELIA	Now, I walk to work.
JO	And?
AMELIA	Leave earlier than I have to.
JO	So?
AMELIA	Leave out while iss still dark.
JO	So what –
AMELIA	so! Today's got 'look at fuckin you' all over it.
JO	And?
AMELIA	Last night got 'look at you' all over it an' all.
	Last night got you and your 'extra-ness' messing it up from the start. You and your – 'what?' – givin it some from the get-go.
JASON	Givin him some from the get-go –
AMELIA	for a change.
JASON	First time for everything.
AMELIA	And there was no need for this mornin to be so damn extra and full up a you, Jo.
JO	But it *is* though Amelia.
AMELIA	*You* made it extra – see! You make it different, Jo, you let it get worse'n what it needs to be. You wanna hit back you make sure you win. You wanna play contender – you stay in the ring. Five minutes a your inspired fuckries last night –

JASON	and he ent gonna let her forget her this morning.
AMELIA	See, there was no need for today to be so… fucked.
JASON	There was no need – yes.
AMELIA	For you to be so… fucked.
JO	Is he sure about 'needs' / is he?
AMELIA	For you to be fuckin with us daily.
JASON	Yeh, iss like –
AMELIA	fuck.
JO	Looks like he's got a need of his own / don't it.
JASON	*Iss* like – wakin up with my back still up to it. On my / side.
JO	(*Dry.*) Looks like he's getting his needs met, Amelia.
	AMELIA *clocks* JO.
JASON	Hard up on it. On my side.
AMELIA	What?
JASON	It's like – waking up with my head on the crick – back up against it, legs lying in fronta me and the wall laughin like it won. Wall all triumphant it's had me against it all night as its trophy.
	Upstairs on my side a that wall that's what it's like.
AMELIA	You're getting worse, Jase.
JASON	That's my night.
AMELIA	See.
JASON	Body bitchin on me that sleeping upright on the ninety degree ent a natural way to catch some zzzs. Thass my mornin.
AMELIA	Should go to your bed shouldn't yer.

JASON

AMELIA   Should go to your bed then – on your side

JASON   what like you do on yourn?

AMELIA   Should –

JASON   go to my bed – like how you take to your sofa
           – is it? Like how you sleepin on your sofa is
           the example I should follow

AMELIA   y'should –

JASON   phone and say I'm strugglin so you, sofa lyin
           – *on your side*, could struggle down the phone
           with me should I?

AMELIA   Phone's upstairs.

JASON   Shoulda phoned and had a one-to-one a
           strugglin together should I?

AMELIA   I left it upstairs

JASON   wouldn'ta rung then.

           Beat.

AMELIA   And you didn't.

JASON   No.

AMELIA   And you don't.

JASON   No.
           I sit up, up here on my side.

AMELIA   I lie down, down there on mine and down
           there I can't hear.

JASON   Chicken shit – makes it cheating, then.

JO   Cheating?

AMELIA   I can't hear is good.

JO   He thinks this is a game?

JASON   You not hearin is easy, so that's your / night.

JO   Tell him this isn't a game / Amelia.

JASON   I heard –

AMELIA   me not hearing her and him is lettin my
           imagination run a marathon, Jase, and that
           don't make it cheating and that don't make it
           easy and that don't make me 'chicken shit' –

JASON   makes you somethin. I *heard*.

AMELIA   And what you doin your side makes you
           somethin an' all –

JASON   least I'm there.

JO   It's not / a game.

JASON   Least I'm up – and / I heard –

JO   Tell him it's / not a game –

AMELIA   Y'not meant to be there!
           And I ent takin shit from you cos you should
           stop listening – *your side* – you should step
           away – *your side*.
           You should stop sittin there – should finish
           your hearing and you should do like what I do
           on my side and gone to you bed.

JASON   Sofa. Ain't it.

AMELIA   That's my night.

AMELIA
JASON

JASON   I shoulda gone to my b-b- / bed.

AMELIA   I know.

JASON   It's my own f-f- / (fault)

AMELIA   I know, Jason.

JASON   …But I hear her Amelia.

AMELIA   I don't wanna know that.

JO   …I do.

JASON   Last night –

JO   I did.

JASON   She hit back…

JO	I did.
AMELIA	See, so – how 'bout, Jo, you tryin t'mek the effort –
JO	I did
AMELIA	some piece a effort to try to shut the fuck up? Bitecha lip or sumthin.
JO	He does that for me.
AMELIA	Holdja tongue.
JO	He does that for me an' all.
AMELIA	Take it like a fuckin man / then –
JO	I do. Don't I.
	You ever wanted – to piss?
	Beat.
AMELIA	No.
JO	Proper get the urge to power piss.
AMELIA	*No.*
JO	Got the ultimate – do it or die, have to go – piss?
	AMELIA *glares coldly at* JO.
	Hold it in for the longest time convincin yourself you don't really wanna – butcha got no choice an' / haveta –
AMELIA	No I haven't.
JO	Has he ever had to piss like that?
AMELIA	He ain't.
JASON	Amelia.
JO	…You sure?
AMELIA	Have ya Jaye?
JASON	No.

AMELIA	See.
JO	Can't hold out – haveta go.
JASON	She shouldn't have gone.
AMELIA	I don't wanna know.
JO	Haveta go before it makes its own route outta me body.
JASON	Amelia –
JO	know I shouldn't go but I have to get up to – this mornin / I have to
AMELIA	I don't need to know, Jo.
JO	If it don't come out as piss come out as yellow tears.
AMELIA	Jo.
JO	And I look beside me to / check –
JASON	*Amelia.*
JO	I sneak a peep, shift a touch, ease up –
JASON	from under.
JO	Ease out
JASON	from beside him
JO	and creep out
JASON	of their bed.
AMELIA	Jason.
JASON	She does –
JO	I do, Amelia.
JASON	I hear, Amelia
JO	I hear him hearing… … I hear him hearing me hear.
	And he knows it.
	Beat. JASON *listens.*
AMELIA	Jason – . Jason –

JASON	what?
AMELIA	Jason –
JASON	ssshhh…
	AMELIA *choopses*.
JO	So when last did you wanna piss like that, then?
JASON	Can still hear her and –
AMELIA	just sleep downstairs.
JASON	Can still / hear them.
AMELIA	Sleep in your downstairs Jase
JASON	I can / hear her –
AMELIA	shut her shit out and – or come over and sleep downstairs with me on my sofa at mine…
JASON	Can hear her even when he's done.
AMELIA	If you wanted.
JASON	Particularly when he's done doin her in –
AMELIA	Jason
JASON	I sit / up –
AMELIA	know you're welcome –
JASON	I sit up back to the / wall –
AMELIA	know you're welcome if you're lookin / company
JASON	back to the wall ear to the glass
AMELIA	and company could do worse than me bein with you / and how 'bout that then?
JASON	Sitting up, back to the wall, ear to the glass – stayin in to listen – stayin up to listen – staying up to listen in on her – and her man – from my side a the wall – again –
AMELIA	please.
JASON	This is my mornin –

AMELIA	I know you won't
JASON	and my mornin before – but now this morning – this mornin my body is proper feelin it and lettin me know
AMELIA	know how long since I've had good / company?
JO	Know how long since I've had good company?
AMELIA	I'd like your company…

Beat.

JO	Company a one and that's too much. Company a two and that makes trouble.
AMELIA	Jason.
JO	Head or tails, which one would you pick?
AMELIA	Jason?

Beat.

JO	Company a one and I do my own head in.
JASON	Company a two and he does it in for her.
AMELIA	And you beggin a third party to hear both that's what's sick.
JO	But you're 'downstairs' entcha. You're in your *downstairs* – entcha A-melia. A-lone. A-gain. You've taken to your sofa, your side, while I'm still wantin with that painful morning piss that won't pass yeh. That I've got to get up to got to get rid of while I'm wonderin – no – *worryin* about wakin him up. *My side.*
AMELIA	(*Dry.*) Yeh. It's a worry.
JO	It is.
JASON	I'm worried about her.
AMELIA	Don't be.

JO	This is my mornin.
AMELIA	Definitely don't be. Why dontcha just go, Jo?
JO	Go and he'll wake – or a lie there and it'll flow / kinda piss.
AMELIA	What-*evah*.
JASON	But she went. Amelia, she *went*.
AMELIA	Big deal.
JO	And it was like –
AMELIA	enough.
JO	Sorta like –
AMELIA	I'm off.
JO	Another morning like that.
JASON	You goin?
AMELIA	I'm off. I'm off out. I went. To the caff.
	Beat.
	I went out to work. You should've come with, Jason.
JASON	…I'm not goin nowhere…
AMELIA JASON JO	
JO	Heard you the other side still, still trying not to be heard…
JASON	I won't go nowhere.
AMELIA	You shoulda come, Jase.
JO	But you've gone, Amelia. You've got up, you've gone out and you have *left*.

	…You ever –
JASON	you ever –
JO	you ever felt to piss like that then?
	…Thought not.
AMELIA	Melody me and my shit. Me and my borin-as-ever shit. Melody make what I'm doin go a little quicker, do what I'm doin quicker still – bored doin what I'm doin – make me forget that I'm doin it.
	Melody me and my borin as ever, pickin up my bottom lip miserably moppin of the other people's floor – shit, Jase.
	The bein there bein invisible – shit.
	And radio land's lettin me down with al their songs sounding like shit and it's doin me in, doin my head right in and maybe what you're hearin, Jaye, maybe what you're hearin where you're at is better'n what I am.
	Beat.
JASON	It's a quiet morning thru the flimsy walls, after a lively night a activity.
JO	Can't hold out haveta go.
JASON	It's a quiet mornin thru the flimsy walls after a lively night a the usual –
JO	fuckin
JASON	usual
JO	fighting
JASON	unusual fighting back – and I – I can't… I c-c-can't…
	JO *winces.* JASON *listens.*
AMELIA	Don't.
	Beat.

	Don't Jase.
JASON	…She's on her hands and knees –
JO	…
JASON	She's nervous as she crawls…
JO	Mmm. (*Nods*.)
AMELIA	Drama queen.
JASON	Him hard-breathin it –
JO	*that's* right.
JASON	But she don't breathe –
JO	yeh.
JASON	Cos she won't breathe –
JO	yes.
JASON	Iss like she can't breathe and I hear –
AMELIA	don't Jase.
JASON	I hear him roll back over as you –
JO	draw the door closed behind me? Well done.
AMELIA	(*Dry*.) Well done. You made it to the bog. Big deal.
JO	You know what Amelia. It is.
JASON	Hear what 'Mel, I'm still sittin there as I was from the night before. I'm still sittin in the same position against that same wall. Shit'd be funny if it wasn't shit eh?
JO	There's a word for people like you.
AMELIA	Word for people like her but she don't use it.
JO	Bucket. Squeeze. Swipe. Why don't you call yourself a cleaner?
	Why don't you call yourself a cleaner? How come you don't call yourself a – not

	even 'domestic assistant', 'facilities hygienist' –
AMELIA	why don't you call / yourself a bitch?
JO	or – *scrubber*.
	Beat.
AMELIA	Something I do, not something I am.
JO	You sure about that?
AMELIA	And what do you call what you are?
JO	Something he does not something I – am.
AMELIA	Somethin you are an' you don't know it.
JO	Likewise.
AMELIA	Something you've become and you don't see it.
JO	I'll call you cleaner for you then, shall I?
AMELIA	Try.
JO	Or you'd prefer – ?
AMELIA	Try me.
	Beat.
JO	(*Dry.*) Bucket isn't it? Then – what? You squeeze it? (*Amused.*) And swipe it with style.
	Well worth getting up for.
	JO *laughs a little, mockingly.*
AMELIA	I'd rather get up to that than get up to greet the bullshit you wake up to.
JO	…So would I.
AMELIA JO	
AMELIA	Just piss Joanne.
JO	So you've never had to check yourself? Never got the art of pissin quietly down pat?

Cos it's all about technique. All about muscles.
All about muscles and release and flow and
speed and angle – you follow me – you've
never had to check how y'piss have ya?
Can tell.

And it's a little lean forward, flow against the
side, little like pouring a good pint, little like
that.
Do someone proud.
Flowin down quite, smooth… and quiet helps.
Don't it.
Quite is good.
Ain't it.
Barely audible's better.
Isn't it.
Helps.
…Doesn't it.

…*Doesn't* it? Jason.

Doesn't it.

JASON   It… d-d-does.

JO   *Thank you.*

It was that sorta mornin.
Aye Amelia?

That's how mine was.
So. You've just been told.

AMELIA   You in no position to tell nobody nuthin
though…
Are ya.

Was yer..?
You weren't in no position to say fuckall, is it,
Jo.
Was it?

JASON   (*Embarrassed.*) N-No.

JO   Burns me as I go and did you hear *that*?
Cos it serves me right for holding it in for so
long.

	Body don't like that Jay, Jay, like that ent healthy.
JASON	Ent healthy sleepin upright, listenin through, you don't have to tell me and I was just about to creak me body up –
JO	I know
JASON	when you crept back in.
JO	Post-piss –
JASON	while he was asleep –
JO	and he wouldn't have known I'd been up at all would he if me body'd behaved and that was the plan and –
JASON	that's the routine and –
JO	that's the normal morning of it and you should know, you should know – I know you know what happens. I know you hear it often enough, I know you know what happens when it's not a good mornin, Jason.
JASON	And this one weren't.
JO	And I had that feelin again as I re-lay there wonderin, after I'd / gone –
JASON	Gone back into / the –
JO	the bedroom.
JASON	Crept back into –
JO	the bed –
JASON	lay back down
JO	next to him, with him deep in the land of nod.
JASON	You thought.
JO	I thought.
	Beat. *Beat.*
	…He's good.
AMELIA	Jason!

JO	You're good.
JASON	I am aren't I Amelia?
AMELIA	Shoulda – you shoulda come, you shoulda come with me Jason. Shoulda seen me skating the floor dry with towels on me feet, like I do. Like I do what usedta make you laugh when you usedta see, remember. When you usedta come. Remember? Remember when you usedta come to the caff and I usedta mop then skate and you usedta see and we usedta laugh and we was in that early together. Remember –
JASON	when I used to come out.
AMELIA	Remember that.
JASON	Just.
	JO *laughs a little mockingly*.
AMELIA	Skate it dry get rid a the pools a too-soapy, too-much, too-wet mop water. Skate it dry do like my Torvill and Dean 'cept didn't know which is which which one's the woman. Who should be Torvill and who should be Dean. We never did know did we, *Jay*? Scatting our 'Bolero' while I'm skatin it dry, singin our bad version while I'm slippin round. And you'd watch. And you'd sing. And I'd dry skate. And then I'd buff.
	And you ever wondered who cleans the floors you trod daily?
JASON	You ever slept upright listenin in at a ninety degrees.
JO	You ever woke up wishin this day to be your last. You ever wondered that?

AMELIA	*No.*
JO	You ever been up for that, Jason?
AMELIA	Leave him alone.
JO	Was up for that, was up for a morning like that.
AMELIA	Leave him alone.
JO	…I had that feelin again…
	Do you see…
JASON	I – I can't / hear…
JO	It still felt like butterflies, Jason. Felt like bad butterflies, deep down in my depths a me, disturbin me as I lay there cold wonderin… waitin…
JASON	I – I…
	JASON *listens.*
AMELIA	Jason.
JASON	What?
AMELIA	Jason!
JASON	What!?
AMELIA	JASE –
JASON	Sssshh!
JO	…Felt like bad butterflies going ballistic. Felt like badness gone wrong – the insides of me carryin on wrong like they're lookin for a way out. And I felt I just wanted to get this day started cos this new morning was already looking old.
AMELIA	Jay.
JO	And I looked across again,
JASON	and y'husband yawned.
AMELIA	Leave Jason *alone* Jo.
JASON	I heard.

JO	And I lay there. Looking up…
JASON	(*Listening.*) What –
	JO *slow rubs her belly.*
	JASON *listens intently.*
	She slowly sighs.
	Aware, she quietly exhales.
JO	And Jason – did you hear that?
AMELIA	That's not the point.
JO	There's only one point if you're listening in.
AMELIA	There's only one reason you're letting him listen –
JO	and you're not invited. …Do it properly, or not at all.
JASON	I will. I am.
AMELIA	Leave him outta it.
JO	This has got nothin to do with you. You wanted this nuthin to do with you. (*Quieter.*) Listen…
JASON	…I hear her yawn –
	Hear him yawn half-awake.
	Hear him yawn and *wait.* And you're quieter, you're nervous with it, you're whisper-askin
	'*Are you awake?*'
AMELIA	'*Are you awake*' – that would irritate me.
JASON	And you're askin the second time –
AMELIA	and your first time would piss me off.
JASON	And you ent even sure – but it's quieter than the first. And I'm not hearin an answer – never hear an answer
JO	cos I'm never gonna get one.

AMELIA   Just you lyin there would piss me off. Juss the
           you a bein you would piss me off. And I'd do
           you meself you lyin there irritatin like that I
           would. Just you bein there's more'n
           justification.

JASON   And you carry on with yer,
           '*I feel funny.*'

AMELIA   That what she said?

JASON   What else?
           Whisperin your – what else?

JO   *I feel hot.*

AMELIA   That what she said? That what woke him up?

JASON   Twitchin under cover like you're restless, pull
           up the twelve-togg a little bit higher – waitin
           on his move.
           Waitin on his mood.
           I am good at this.

           Silence.

JASON   You –

JO   wait.

           Pause.

JASON   Cos then your dirty dancin-belly-butterfly-
           come-down-burn, revealed itself as...

JO   (*Quietly.*) blood.

           Beat.

AMELIA   This is not a good morning.

JASON   And it's not a good morning.

AMELIA   This one weren't.

JASON   And it coulda been

AMELIA   but now it ent.

JASON   And you turned it –

AMELIA   you turned it – *you* turned it

JASON   you turned it when you s-s-ss-s–

AMELIA	*said*
JO	…I'm bleeding.
JASON	…*Thass* what woke him up.
	Beat.
	Thank you.
JO	
JASON	
JO	
JASON	I creak up. Stand up to get up, getting up to get into position two. Second position to listen to her, better position to listen to yer. And you thought it was nerves. You thought it was s-s-somethin else. Your dancin – diggin
AMELIA	dirty butterfly fuckries.
JASON	The damage had been done from doing you before.
AMELIA	And from before that
JASON	burning from the inside out.
AMELIA	And from before that an' all –
JASON	burning you on their way down – and today ent even hardly started. And you don't haveta tell me nuthin – you don't tell me nuthin – you don't haveta tell me that's the kinda mornin it is – you don't tell me a thing cos I hear – heard you and you was –
JO	screaming.
JASON	And screamin like that. Like that ent healthy. J-J-Jo.
JO	I panicked.
JASON	And you was bleeding all / down –
JO	I – Jason –
JASON	*you* made the morning different like that –
JO	then he –

JASON	and you was still screaming / Jo.
JO	then he –
AMELIA	see why I left?
JO	Then he shut me up.

Beat.

AMELIA	See why I left?
JASON	Then what did you say?
AMELIA	And who asked you to go get brave last night? Who asked you to brave up yourself last night and fuck up all a we mornin?
JO	You know what I said I don't need to repeat it, you know what I said – I do know you know.
JASON	What did you say then?
AMELIA	Not so brave now are ya?
JASON	I want you to say.
JO	I know you *heard*. I know *what* you heard.
JASON	*Say it…*
JO	…
AMELIA	Where's the slap-back-bitch-givin-it-the-mouth now? She for one night only then?
JASON	*Say it.*
JO	'…I am sorry.'

AMELIA *shakes her head in disgust.*

AMELIA	'*Sorry*?' Yeh. You proper are. You're proper pitiful, Joanne. And was 'sorry' really cuttin it?
JASON	No. No, it's not. It wasn't.

Beat.

	Thank you.
	Pause.
JO	I knew from the morning dawning that today was gonna kick.
AMELIA	Stop it.
JO	And it did. I knew from the reluctant-wakin, eye-glue poppin, dead-/leg stretching of the meeting of the…
AMELIA	Yeh yeh yeh. You've said.
JASON	…But this beautiful morning's looking old and stale and worn and d-d-dirty like yesterday, already…
	Beat.
	S'lookin like you J-Jo.
JO	(*Mocking.*) Jer-Jer-Jer-Jo. Know you're there cos the wall shudders with yer.
JASON	Rest your head against it and I'll wh-whisper thru in your ear.
JO	Wouldja?
JASON	…I did…
	Beat.
JO	What would you wear – wondering this was your last day – start of a day like that?…
	Beat.
AMELIA	Nothin.
	Beat.
JO	I wore black to mark it. I wore black. Very lacy.
AMELIA	You would, you would.
JO	I did.

AMELIA	I know.
JASON	I wouldn'ta bought you that.
JO	Not old. Not holey. Not worn. I wore charcoal-black, bikini-line BHS-brand new-box-fresh baggies. And he always had taste.
MALEIA	If you like that sorta thing.
JASON	I wouldn'ta made you wear that.
JO	Thing is, that's what he brought across, 'Melia. And that's the thing. And that's the thing. Things he threw across, Jason – 'cross the room at me
JASON	I heard –
JO	and he always had taste and he's fully awake and he's out from under and he's demanding me to… what is it – what – *what was it*, Jase..?
JASON	'…get up.'
JO	Ahhh, and what do I shout back… *go on*…
JASON	'…it weren't my f-f-fault.'
JO	What do I shout back?
AMELIA	In between ya screamin.
JASON	'It weren't my / f-fault.'
JO	Yeh but Jase, how do I say it without the retardation?
JASON	F-f-f- / fault.
AMELIA	Leave him alone.
JO	And *then* what? C'mon. How good are you? Don't play shy now J., cos shy don't suit –

JASON	'…weren't mine neither.'
JO	weren't his what?
JASON	'Weren't mine n-neither'
JO	weren't his *what* neither?
JASON	'F-f- / f-f…'
AMELIA	JASON!
JO	Believe him didja? *Say it!*
AMELIA	Jo!
JASON	F-f- / f-f–
JO	Believe *him* didja? That it wasn't his *fault*? *Say it*!
JASON	F-f-fuck off.
JO	And you were gonna whisper me choice words a wisdom to help me out?
JASON	You was messin up the twelve-togg. You was soakin through your sheets. You'd gone through to the m-m-mattress. I heard – but it weren't your fault… J-Jo. *He listens* JO *laughs a little. Mocking.* And you was still screamin.
JO	I was.
JASON	You can't stop.
JO	I didn't.
AMELIA	You won't stop.
JO	I don't.
JASON	Till he stopped you.
JO	Someone had to.
JASON	Why like that?

AMELIA	Someone had to.
JASON	Why like that?
JO	*You* never saw. You only *heard*. *You* don't know.
JASON	Know what I know you make me hear –
JO	you hear what I wantcha to.
AMELIA	See.
JASON	Butcha don't know if I'm – lis-listenin – do yer?
JO	You will. You do. Y'can't help yourself.
JASON	Can.
JO	Y'can't
JASON	I can.
JO	You don't.
JASON	I could.
JO	You couldn't. You won't. I know. I know you. And you certainly can't help me can yer?
JASON	You-you-you –
JO	'you! You! You!' You – *ever*? Is it?!
	JO *laughs a little mockingly.*
	Beat.
JASON	You know if that was me with you… wouldn't have quieted you like that –
JO	that be you still bein my next-door knight in shining armour. That be you still being my next-door knight that never moves a muscle that loves listenin in and whispers words a comfort that get lost passing through. That be you or whatever part your wishing yourself to play in y'audio version a my mornin – Jason.

JASON	Know if that was me with you, woulda treated you c-c-careful, Jo, gentle like – glass hearin the fragile / state you in –
JO	You in position that you never saw nothin though entcha? Didja. You're in the position, *Jase*, that you couldn't do a thing? Could you?
JASON	Know if that was me with you / wouldn't have –
JO	oh you would.
JASON	Woulda handled you –
JO	you wouldn't.
AMELIA	I wouldn't.
JASON	Woulda treated you / gentle –
JO	You couldn't.
JASON	I / could –
AMELIA	You couldn't handle that. You couldn't handle that. Could ya? You wouldn't have clue yeh? You couldn't handle 'gentle' if 'gentle' was –
JO	listenin in next door to me?
JASON	Hearin you – / the fragile state you –
JO	You in – yeh? You – what? You in – what? *You*, in position (*Mocking.*) 'ter-ter-two', Jason. Head against the wall, pressed up hearing whatever leaks through. Jason. Is it. Is it? That's as good as you position two gets. (*Mocking.*) Ger-ger-ger-got. Jason. Isn't it? And position three don't exist. Does it? Does it…?

Or, is it that, *that* makes the wall shudder with
yer then.
Is it your '*position three*' that I can hear
clearly comin through…?
That's when I know you're there for sure, see.
Getting your hand dirty.
Jason.

And you'd have shut me up the same way as
he did… only you'd have been, 'positioning
three' freely with it.
Jay.

This morning's as dirty as you are.

Pause.

There's a word for people like you.

AMELIA   There's a word for people like *you*.

And there is a word for people like you.
Jason.

JASON   …There's a word for people like him and how
he s-s- / shut her up –

AMELIA   Didja?
Jason? Didja?

JASON   No.

JO   You fuckin liar –

AMELIA   Jason?

JASON   N-N-No.

JO
JASON
JO

JO *and* JASON *eyeball each other*
challengingly. He refuses to speak on.

JO   (*Triumphantly.*) Thank you.

AMELIA
JO
AMELIA

	JASON *holds no eye contact.*
	Beat.
	Pause.
AMELIA	Bitch.
JO	And?
	Beat. *Beat.*
	Pause.
AMELIA	Jase…? Jason…
	JO *laughs a little at them.*
	This morning scares me, Jo.
JO	We're speaking? We're speaking?
JASON	This morning sucks. And I'm still shaking and you've been shut up and maybe I coulda phoned like I should, but I forgot I didn't have your number. And maybe I regret I never called round like I could but I forgot I don't even know yer. And I'm still next door. And I know you knew. And I knew you were listening me like I listen you.
	…You got me been there for d-d-days.
AMELIA	You got him addicted, Jo.
JO	Why don't you just leave?
AMELIA	You got him doin like you –
JASON	you got me not eating. Not sleeping. You got my ear against our wall –
JO	why don't you walk?
AMELIA	You got him hooked, Jo.
JO	Even to another room.

AMELIA	You got him so I don't see him…
JASON	You got me d-d-disgusted with myself daily
AMELIA	you got him where you wanted him, Jo.
JASON	Disgusting myself daily.
JO	You disgust me.
AMELIA	You got him that he don't come out. You got him that I can't find him.
JO	Why don't you *go*?
JASON	Hourly disgusted and disgusted I'm still here and enjoying my disgust and knowing I'll s-s- / stay.
JO	Disgusting ent it.
AMELIA	You knew he was listening –
JO	did I?
AMELIA	You knew he'd / hear –
JO	*And?*
AMELIA	*And* – you knew what you wanted him to hear, knowing he would stay and you knew what that would do.
JO	So?
AMELIA	So why don't *you* go?
JO	Ask *him*.
AMELIA	*Why didn't you go Jase?*
JASON	Ent that eas-ease- / easy…
JO	Ent that easy. Is it. *Pause.* Waitin on me to apologise are ya? Waiting on me to apologise for getting you up are yer? …Waiting on me to apologise for keeping you up is it. waiting on me to –

AMELIA	no.
JO	Are y'waiting on me to –
AMELIA	I wouldn't wait on you for nothing, Jo.
JO	
AMELIA	
JO	
JASON	
JO	What are you waiting for then?

Beat.

…No.
I won't apologise for it.
Thank you.

But I left.

AMELIA	Him? I don't think so.
JO	I left.
AMELIA	Him is it?
JO	I left – the flat. I went. I went out.
JASON	You – crawled out. Jo.

JO *quietly mouths a dry 'thank you' in*
JASON's *direction.*

JO	Miss me then? What part a your anatomy missed me then?

Beat.

AMELIA	Whyja come? By the caff – why did you come? And after I'd told you not to. After I'd asked you nice. Whyja come? Why did you come? Why did you *come*?

JASON *starts to cry.*

JO	Did you Jason?

Beat.

Didja come?
Didja?

Beat.

Wanker.

JASON   …Amelia…

JO *watches* JASON *bemusedly.*
AMELIA *avoids his gaze.*

Amelia.

AMELIA   What?

JASON   Amelia –

AMELIA   Jason?

Beat.

JASON   Ame–

AMELIA   shhh.

Shut up.

Beat.

JO   …Listen.

Music track plays out.

Epilogue

*Early a.m. In the moment. In the morning. In the café. The café
is extremely shiny, clinically clean.*
*There is a large, elaborate very shiny coffee machine on the
counter. There is an open flask on a table/chair combo with a
part-drunk flask cup of coffee beside it.*
There is a smell of yesterday's coffee about the place.
Outside it rains. It is still dark.
JO *is weak. She is damaged. She is bleeding. She is wet. She is
defiant. (She looks a mess.)*
The tinny café radio is on, pumping out pop music.

AMELIA *buffs her floor intensely with a cumbersome machine.*
(AMELIA *also has 'softs' on her feet for that extra sheen.*)
She gets bored.

Without looking up, AMELIA *senses* JO *is in.*

AMELIA	Get out.
JO	
AMELIA	Shut up Jo, I don't need to hear –
JO	Amelia.
AMELIA	I don't need to see…
JO	I'm in.
AMELIA	And we are closed.
JO	
AMELIA	Don't thank me, there's a sign.
JO	Fuck you.
AMELIA	Don't bother thank me – 'ignorant'.
JO	But I'm here now.
AMELIA	Yeh. Again. You are.
	Beat.

	Jesus Jo, man.
	You look – a fuckin state.
JO	Thank you.
AMELIA	Y'look worse –
JO	thank you.
AMELIA	This is the worst.
JO	…Thanks.
	Beat.
AMELIA	And whatja come for?
JO	Walked.
AMELIA	Howja get here?
JO	To see you.
AMELIA	Whatja want, Jo?
JO	…Nuthin.
AMELIA	And 'nuthin's' got my name on it is it.
JO	
AMELIA	'Nuthin' happens to be where I'm at – is it.
JO	…
AMELIA	Again, is it?… Yeh?
	Nothing's here for yer, is what I toldja – is there. Is it? Nuthin I can do yu for and – and – look at the state a yer, y'shouldn't even be out – look how y'look nowhere near ready to reach.
JO	But Amelia –
AMELIA	you look a fuckin state.
JO	But Amelia –
AMELIA	you got no good God reason to be out Jo – you got no right to be out here *Jo* –
JO	see but that's the point, Amelia, now I'm in.
	Be nice.

AMELIA	Nice don't getchu nowhere does it?
JO	I wouldn't know.
AMELIA	Nice don't count for shit.
JO	I wouldn't know.
AMELIA	You wouldn't know nice if it come and smacked you round the face.
JO	It did.
AMELIA	Shit. You seen yourself…
JO	'Shit.'
AMELIA	You taken a good look?
JO	Have I?
AMELIA	Y'look…
JO	like I don't know.
AMELIA	…You look as bad as what my floor looks good. Looked. Good. Look at my / floor…
JO	You're lookin at me like I'm lettin the side down.
AMELIA	Are ya?
JO	You're lookin at me like I'm –
AMELIA	well you tell me.
JO	Lookin / at me like –
AMELIA	Look what you're doin – where you're drippin – look at my floor!
JO	Look at me.
AMELIA	No.
JO	Look at me.
AMELIA	Wha'for?
JO	Look what he / done –

AMELIA	Why? Jo?
JO	Let me show you *Amelia* –
AMELIA	nah, cos – again – thank you – and – no. / So.
JO	Amelia –
AMELIA	I don't wanna see. I don't need to see. I don't have to see – you. Yeh. So, no.

Pause.

JO	Not this, I never.

Beat.

AMELIA	Neither did I.

Beat.

JO	Not this I wouldn't.

Beat.

AMELIA	Neither would I. You're trouble you are, y'know that.
JO	I'm here.
AMELIA	Big capital T, you know that?
JO	But I am here.
AMELIA	Big bag a double / trouble.
JO	You sound like him.
AMELIA	You look like a new sport.
JO	You've taken his lines –
AMELIA	and what have you taken? What you still takin? What you gonna go home take more of and don't even feel no way –

JO *just about makes to move.*

And don't sit –

JO	– down?
AMELIA	*Don't.*
JO	I won't.

AMELIA	Don't. Everything's just clean.
JO	I see.
AMELIA	Everything's just done.
JO	I know.
AMELIA	I juss done doing it all.
JO	Everything's all shiny.
AMELIA	Everything's all clean, everything's all ready. Everything's all done and prepared and washed and stacked and sparklin and ready for *them* to start *their* day, Jo, when *they* come in, and not for *you* to spoil up when *you* start yours by staggerin in here when you're ready. See.
JO	My day starts as early as yours.
AMELIA	My day starts because a yours.
JO	My day starts / with –
AMELIA	I don't wanna know.
	Pause.
JO	…Should I shut the – ?
AMELIA	That be on your way out then?
JO	…Should I close the / door?
AMELIA	And mark it as well? Oh no.
	Beat. AMELIA *gently, reluctantly closes the door.* *And locks it.* AMELIA *straightens up the 'closed' sign.*
AMELIA	This is what I'm doing from tomorrow. This is what I shoulda done from today.
JO	I think – it'll be open.
AMELIA	From tomorrow it won't.
JO	It'll be open.
AMELIA	I'm keeping it back locked Jo.

JO	Is it.
AMELIA	An' you can knock and knock march on up here and do what the frigg y'want but I won't be opening it.
JO	Is it.
AMELIA	You'll be out. I'll be in. You'll be there. I'll be here. In here blanking yer.
JO	What, like now?
AMELIA	Try me.
JO	I have.
AMELIA	Try me.
JO	I did.
AMELIA	Try me again.
JO	And I'm in. See.

Beat.

AMELIA	Try me tomorrow, Joanne.
JO	…Won't be here then.
AMELIA	That a promise is it?
JO	Yeh.
AMELIA	Y'look shit.

AMELIA *looks to the floor at* JO*'s reflection.*

Y'look shit twice.

JO *doesn't look.*
AMELIA *watches* JO, *literally dripping blood from between her legs.* JO*'s dripping on the floor becomes unacceptable.*
AMELIA *exits.*
She returns with a wad of paper towels and an opened pack of sanitary towels.

AMELIA	Catch.

She gently throws the sanitary towel pack to
JO, *who makes no effort to catch it. It hits her.*
She doesn't flinch.

Beat.

AMELIA *starts to open up and lay paper*
towels unapologetically around JO*'s feet*
where she is dripping and marking the floor.

AMELIA	Satisfied?
JO	…Don't touch though.
AMELIA	Won't touch –
JO	don't touch me 'Mel –
AMELIA	do I ever and I'm not.
JO	You won't –
AMELIA	I'm not.
JO	I don't want you –
AMELIA	I don't wanna –
JO	touching me –
AMELIA	think I wanna? *Alright.* …I haven't. See. So what am I sposed to do? What is it I'm sposed to do? …Shit. What is it you come for? What is it you keep coming for? What is it you want?

AMELIA *watches her bleed.*

And what's coming out?
You?

JO	Me.
AMELIA	Only you?
JO	Only me.

AMELIA *carefully lays a paper towel path towards the toilets.*

AMELIA   You sure?

Beat.
JO *nods.*

AMELIA   Here.

AMELIA *hands some paper towels to* JO.

Run go touch yourself.
And mind my – floor.

AMELIA *goes to hand the pack of sanitary towels to* JO. JO *does not take them.*

And do somethin useful with these… y'need to sort yourself out… yeh… fix up.

JO   Sorry about your floor.

AMELIA   So am I.

JO   Sorry 'bout your floor, noticed it was nice.

AMELIA   Yeh. It *was* weren't it.

JO   Sorry boutcha shine –

AMELIA   yeh – you've said

JO   sorry / boutcha –

JO *is in pain.*

AMELIA   sorry boutcha self – y'need to shut up and be appreciated if you don't sit –

JO   can't sit –

AMELIA   (of) course.

AMELIA *proceeds to lay a path of paper towels to a chair and table combo. She lays more paper towels over the table and over the chair.*

Very slowly and painfully she half-guides half-watches JO*'s attempts at sitting, which is agony, but eventually successful.*
(*This is part routine for both of them.*)

| JO | You done something different then? You've done somethin nice for 'em? Is this some occasion? You gone that extra mile have you? You have, you've pushed the boat out to make a good impression, trying t'get in their good books – or just to stay there – what is it – you get a gold star or something for how much shine the floor's showing?… |

Notice things like that I do.
S'a woman's eye.
Detail. Got the eye for it. You and me both.
Notice things like that don't we.
Bet they won't.

Beat.

I'm impressed.

Beat.

Did I say that I was impressed?

Beat.

What you do's impressive.
And least you're gettin outta your house.

AMELIA	Least I am.
JO	Least you got somewhere to go.
AMELIA	Least I have.
JO	…Least you got that.

AMELIA *sits and sips from her (flask) coffee.*
JO *watches.*
AMELIA *offers.*

No.

AMELIA *drinks.*

Thirsty though.

| AMELIA | I don't do service. |
| JO | Cuppa somethin warm 'n' wet. All milk and froth – |

AMELIA	don't do service do I. I won't do service.
JO	Still not allowed to touch their stuff? Still wishin you could?
AMELIA	Still wishin you weren't here – still wishin you'd fuck off –
JO	I'm thirsty.
AMELIA	Least a your worries.
JO	I want a drink.
AMELIA	Little thirst ent gonna hurtcha.
JO	It does though
AMELIA	'll blend in with the rest then won't it.

Beat.

JO	I'm not beggin it for free. I wouldn't do that. I wouldn't do that would I? Never done that before.
AMELIA	Ent never made you coffee before.
JO	I not askin it for nuthin is all.
AMELIA	You playing proud now?
JO	I wouldn't know.
AMELIA	Are you playin proud?
JO	Wouldn't know how.
AMELIA	I think you are.
JO	You tell me.
AMELIA	God don't like proud.
JO	God don't like ugly.
AMELIA	Keep going…
JO	God don't like me.
AMELIA	Nah, it's I who don't like you, Jo.
JO	There you go sounding like him again Amelia. …Go on…

AMELIA	They'll be in to open up soon.
JO	Go on… I know you know how.

Beat.

AMELIA	They got their own little coffee-machine routines.
JO	Go on. I know you wanna.
AMELIA	Their own little ways a doin it.
JO	Impress me.
AMELIA	…Stand there and do the noises sometimes, don't I. Style it out my way. Stand there and do the noises and make like I even got a queue an' everything. Sometimes.

When I'm on me own. In on me own. Here. Do it how I seen it been done, how I seen them do it, make like I'm all stressed like how they do. 'Cept I'd do it better. And I watch 'em from the sly – from the outside in – when my shift's over when daylight hits and the daytime people come in and do their thing.

When I'm here on me own.

Make out like it's the lunchtime rush and I'm dealin with it single-handed – on me jack – and there's a little bit a the 'queue-rage' goin down that I'm tryinta passify and I'm imaginin pumpin out cups a 'this' – takeout 'thats' – grande whatevers and – .

Beat.

Sometimes I piss about like that.
Fuck about like that.

Fucked ent it.

JO
AMELIA
JO

AMELIA   …When they come Jo, when they open up,
I'm gonna go. Gonna go back home, I'm
gonna skip up my stairs, gonna visit my
bedroom, gonna turn off my radio – I'm
gonna – might even take a little *lie*-down – Jo,
gonna turn everything off and take this as the
'quiet' it is while I know you're out and
about.

AMELIA *makes to clean up some of the
paper towels on the floor. She doesn't notice
that she has* JO's *blood on her own feet* (*softs*)
*so every step makes a bloody footprint.
She becomes part of her own problem.*

JO   You really make the coffee machine noises
with your mouth, fakin it…?

AMELIA
JO
AMELIA

JO   Do yer? I think that's cute that is.
Really. I do.
(*Dry.*) I think that's really… *somethin* –

JO *suddenly vomits over the floor, where there
are no paper towels.*

AMELIA   Jesus Jo man.

AMELIA *notices her own prints.*

What's the matter with you?

JO   Uhhh…
…I'll be alright.

AMELIA   Oh Jesus.
Shit.

JO   I will –

AMELIA   shit

JO   I'll be fine –

AMELIA   *fuck.* / Jo.

JO	Thanks.
	I'm okay.
	Did I say I was sorry boutcha floor?
	I am.
AMELIA	Fuck you Jo –
JO	I really am and 'don't thank me' –
AMELIA	and fuck him too… y'need to stay – y'need to stay – y'need to stay away, away from me – from me, from Jase, from me, from here. From him. Fuck you Jo. You need to stay away and I am gonna keep the door locked back from tomorrow
JO	won't matter won't be here then.
AMELIA	Y'said that yesterday –
JO	you ever woke up wonderin this was / your last day
AMELIA	said that the day before an' all.
JO	This one's it.
AMELIA	You're gonna haveta keep away.
JO	Today is it.
AMELIA	You're gonna haveta keep your distance.
JO	This has to be it
AMELIA	cos I'll be keeping mine.
JO	I want this to be it
AMELIA	but you'll be back though. You'll be back, Jo. You'll be back here –
JO	this is it
AMELIA	cos you *go* back. Cos you do.
	So, we're fucked.
	Beat.

JO	…I want this day to be over.
AMELIA	And I'm askin you nice.
JO	Want this day to be over –
AMELIA	I'm sayin it *nice* –
JO	need this mornin to finish.
AMELIA	I'm bein nice to you cos I ent gonna ask you again. I'm not gonna ask you nicely again am I?

AMELIA *draws a clean glass of crisp water.*

JO	Not what I want. Not what I want. It's not what I want.

AMELIA *gives it to* JO.

I won't drink it.

AMELIA	…I know thatcha will.
JO	I won't.
AMELIA	I know you tho.
JO	…I know you more.
AMELIA	And I know you more'n that, don't I.
JO AMELIA	
JO	This mornin ent had nuthin good to offer up, y'know? It started off shit – y'know? And it don't finish yet and I can't wait for the afternoon to come.

JO *drinks*.

AMELIA	Jesus. You ever –
JO	I can't wait.
AMELIA	You ever woken up of / a –
JO	I proper can't wait.
AMELIA	Jo?

JO	Amelia…
AMELIA	Jo… *Jo –*
JO	ssshh.

End.

generations

generations was first performed as a Platform performance at the National Theatre, London, on 30 June 2005. The cast was as follows:

GRANDDAD	Jeffrey Kissoon
NANA	Golda John
MAMA	Rakie Ayola
DAD	Danny Sapani
GIRLFRIEND (OLDER SISTER)	Sharlene Whyte
JUNIOR SISTER	Nikki Amuka-Bird
BOYFRIEND	Seun Shote

With members of the African Voices Choir

Director	Sacha Wares

Characters

BOYFRIEND
GIRLFRIEND (*Older Sister*)
JUNIOR SISTER
MAMA
DAD
NANA
GRANDDAD
…*and a* CHOIR

All characters are Black South Africans. Nana and Granddad are Mama's parents.

The conversations are fluid and constant, although some may be happening in different time frames between certain characters.

Names without dialogue indicate active silences between those characters.

/ marks where dialogue starts to overlap.

The choir/live vocals should start prior to, then underscore parts of the text. A Black South African choir would be great.

Pre-show songs used in 2007: As audience enter the choir sing:

'X'Ethewabonakala', 'Dlamini', 'Digkomo', 'Thongo Lam', 'Noikhokhele', 'The Ameni'.

Pre-show songs were not laments.

Pre-show songs may be changed but should be traditional Black South African content, not sung in English.

Prologue: The Names

Onstage CHOIR *sing with the following names called out, repeated and lamented over. They are not singing in English. (You may or may not get through the list – or may need to repeat it…)*

1. *Sabata*   *'Sabata': Another leaves us, another has gone.*

2. *Ketso*   *'Ketso': Another leaves us, another has gone.*

3. *Oliver*   *'Oliver': Another leaves us, another has gone.*

4. *Josiah*   *'Josiah' (Etc.)*

5. *Kobie*   *'Kobie'*

6. *Clements*   *'Clements'*

7. *Jongilizwe*   *'Jongilizwe'*

8. *Nyathi*   *'Nyathi'*

9. *George*   *'George'*

10. *Moses*   *'Moses'*

11. *Bernard*   *'Bernard'*

12. *Bantu*   *'Bantu'*

13. *TJ*   *'TJ'*

14. *Leonora*   *'Leonora'*

15. *Mama Gee*   *'Mama Gee'*

16. *Nomafu*   *'Nomafu'*

17. *Maulvi*   *'Maulvi'*

18. *Selma*   *'Selma'*

19. *Kolane*   *'Kolane'*

20. *Zwelibhangile*
       'Zwelibhangile'

21. *Kwezi*   *'Kwezi'*

22. *Mary*   *'Mary'*

23. *Ludwe*   *'Ludwe'*

24. *Patricia*   *'Patricia'*

25. *Dumisani*   *'Dumisani'*

26. *Kolade*   *'Kolade'*

27. *Mannie*   *'Mannie'*

28. *Elias*   *'Elias'*

29. *Solomon*   *'Solomom'*

30. *Nana*   *'Nana'*

31. *Potlako*   *'Potlako'*

32. *Lindiwe*   *'Lindiwe'*

33. *Mpho*   *'Mpho'*

34. *Duma*   *'Duma'*

35. *Phyllis*   *'Phyllis'*

36. *Sefako*   *'Sefako'*

37. *Zaccheus*   *'Zaccheus'*

38. *Leleti*   *'Leleti'*

39. *Nkosana*   *'Nkosana'*

40. *Vanessa*   *'Vanessa'*

41. *Lerato*   *'Lerato'*

42. *Nthato*   *'Nthato'*

43. *Zachariah*   *'Zachariah'*

44. *Ambrose*   *'Ambrose'*

45. *Celie*   *'Celie'*

46. *Tsepo*   *'Tsepo'*

47. *Robert*   *'Robert'*

48. *Kipizane*   *'Kipizane'*

49. *Nandi*   *'Nandi'*

50. *Tebogo*   *'Tebogo'*

51. *Nkululeko*   *'Nkululeko'*

52. *Siboniso*   *'Siboniso'*

53. *Duma*   *'Duma'*

54. *Deliwe*   *'Deliwe'*

55. *Thandani*   *'Thandani'*

56. *Anele*   *'Anele'*

57. *Xolani Nkosi Johnson*
                     'Xolani Nkosi Johnson'

58. *Makgatho Mandela*
                     'Makgatho Mandela'

Scene One

The lament and the list of names continues from Prologue. The names fade, leaving the wordless melody only.

The melody stops. Snap into:

GIRLFRIEND   Askin me –

JNR SISTER   he asked her –

GIRLFRIEND   he asked me if / I –

JNR SISTER   Mama, he asked her if she / could –

GIRLFRIEND   askin me if I could –

BOYFRIEND   ' – able.
You are.
You are – able.'

JNR SISTER   Able?

GIRLFRIEND   Thinks he can ask me

JNR SISTER   thinks he can sweet you –

GIRLFRIEND   thinks he can sweetmouth me with:

JNR SISTER   sweetmouth her with –

BOYFRIEND   'you are – you is – you do – you able – you
look you look like you able – to have the
ability the capability the capacity, the
complete… about you – '

JNR SISTER   to what –

BOYFRIEND   'to… to…'

GIRLFRIEND   'to what?'

JNR SISTER   That's not gonna work.

GIRLFRIEND   He thinks that's going to work?

JNR SISTER   Mama, he asked her if she could cook

BOYFRIEND	' – the aptitude the talent the touch.'
GIRLFRIEND	'The touch?'
BOYFRIEND	'The – you are – you is – you do – you do got – the touch… The lightness of touch – the sweetness of touch – sweetness of your touch – the talent to touch a little – '
JNR SISTER	oh God –
BOYFRIEND	'touch a little of – '
GIRLFRIEND	'oh God – '
BOYFRIEND	'of sweetness… You do – you is – you are – look at you… Look how – look how *sweet* – how sweet the touch – '
JNR SISTER	is this workin?
BOYFRIEND	'How sweet that would – touch – '
GIRLFRIEND	'*what*?'
BOYFRIEND	'your touch would – '
	JNR SISTER *kisses her teeth*.
BOYFRIEND	' – could that… taste…The composure – '
JNR SISTER	'what did he say?'
BOYFRIEND	'The control – '
JNR SISTER	'don't mind him – '
MAMA	he asked you if you could cook?
BOYFRIEND	'The calm, the control, the composure you contain – '
JNR SISTER	to what?
BOYFRIEND	'The capabilities you must have – '
GIRLFRIEND	'to what?'
BOYFRIEND	'To carry out your – '
JNR SISTER	oh God

BOYFRIEND	'your – culinary…'
MAMA	Oh God
BOYFRIEND	'to – *cook*.'
DAD	I asked you if you could cook –
MAMA	you knew I could cook –
DAD	can she / cook?
JNR SISTER	I can cook
MAMA	which is why you asked me – you knew – he knew –
DAD	she can't cook
MAMA	you knew. Why did you ask? He knew – he knew before he asked – he asked because he did know –
JNR SISTER	Dada, I can.
MAMA	Mama ask him –
NANA	why did you ask?
DAD	She looked like she could eat.
	GRANDDAD *is amused*.
MAMA	*That's* your father
DAD	a well-fed woman. *That's* my wife.
NANA	*My* daughter –
GRANDDAD	our well-fed daughter.
JNR SISTER	I can cook
DAD	but can she?
	GIRLFRIEND *says nothing*.
JNR SISTER	She can't
DAD	she doesn't cook.
JNR SISTER	She won't cook.
MAMA	I coached her to cook.

JNR SISTER	I coached her to cook.
MAMA	Coached them to cook.
DAD	Why doesn't she cook?
JNR SISTER	Cos she can't –
GIRLFRIEND	Mama cooks. I eat. Mama cooks, what I eat.
MAMA	They learnt their cooking capabilities from me.
NANA	*I* coached you to cook –
MAMA	I –
NANA	I did. I was the cooker – you was the cookless – I was the cooker who coached the cookless. I coached you to / cook –
GRANDDAD	You couldn't cook.
GIRLFRIEND	Nana couldn't cook?
DAD	Your mother couldn't / cook?
MAMA	Course she could cook –
NANA	– I couldn't cook?
MAMA	Mama could cook
NANA	I couldn't / cook?
MAMA	Dada, Mama could cook. Course she could cook – she coached me – and he knows it
GRANDDAD	you couldn't cook either.
GIRLFRIEND JNR SISTER	
GRANDDAD	I coached her. I coached her too. *That's* your mother.
JNR SISTER	Mama couldn't cook?
MAMA	Shut up.
GRANDDAD	She was a bad learner.

NANA	…Don't mind him. Don't pay him no mind.
MAMA NANA MAMA	
GIRLFRIEND	He asked me if I could cook, Mama –
GRANDDAD	he asked *her* – if she could *cook*?
	GRANDDAD *is amused.*
MAMA	This is how they start –
NANA	oh.
JNR SISTER	Sis, 'this is how they start'
DAD	have to start somewhere –
MAMA	oh.
	GRANDDAD *laughs.*
	This is how your father started with me.
NANA	This is how your father started with me.
MAMA	This is how your father flirted with me. This is how your father's flirting first started with me
DAD	still working out where to start with you
MAMA	*eh?*
	GRANDDAD *is amused.*
NANA	He looked like he needed a meal. You looked like you needed a meal.
DAD	I needed a meal.
GRANDDAD	He looked like I did.
NANA	You needed more than a meal
DAD	she looked well-fed.
GRANDDAD	Got more than a meal –
MAMA	eh – what?
GRANDDAD	Got more than what I asked for.

JNR SISTER	*What*?
	DAD *is amused.*
GRANDDAD	Got more than –
NANA	don't mind him – don't pay your grandfather no mind – he don't know what he's sayin
GRANDDAD	"I don't know what I'm sayin"?
NANA	He don't know what he's rememberin.
GRANDDAD	"I don't know what I'm rememberin"?
GIRLFRIEND	I'm sayin 'do I look like someone who can't?'
BOYFRIEND	'You look like – '
JNR SISTER	'does she look like someone who can't?'
BOYFRIEND	'You look like someone who could – '
GIRLFRIEND	'do I look like someone who couldn't?'
JNR SISTER	'She doesn't look like someone who / couldn't.'
BOYFRIEND	'You look like someone who should.'
GIRLFRIEND	'I know I don't look like someone who couldn't – '
JNR SISTER	'she don't look like – '
GIRLFRIEND	(*To* SISTER.) *shut up* – (*To* BOYFRIEND.) '…I know I don't look like someone who couldn't…'
BOYFRIEND	'You look like someone who would…'
MAMA	Oh God
BOYFRIEND	' – would cook. Who is able… who has the talent…'
	DAD *is amused.*
DAD	He has the mouth
NANA	he has the mouth.
MAMA	You had the mouth

DAD	I was better.
GIRLS	Were you?
DAD	Still am.
JNR SISTER	Was he?
GRANDDAD	I was better.
NANA	Oh God. Don't mind / him.
GRANDDAD	I was something
NANA	he thought he was / something.
GRANDDAD	still am something
NANA	still thinks he's something
GRANDDAD	she knows exactly what kinda / something –
NANA	don't mind him –
GRANDDAD	forgotten nothing
NANA	forgotten everything
GRANDDAD	and neither have you.
NANA GRANDDAD	
MAMA	Don't mind them.
BOYFRIEND	'The – '
GIRLFRIEND	'what?'
BOYFRIEND	'The – '
JNR SISTER	'what?'
BOYFRIEND	'The – '
NANA	what did he say?
BOYFRIEND	'The – what can I say… The what is there to say? The what is there to say about – you?'
MAMA	Oh God. Mouth.

BOYFRIEND	'The – what is there to say about you?'
DAD	Mouth.
	CHOIR: *The melody of the lament restarts hummed under the following:*
BOYFRIEND	'The what is there left to say about you?
	BOYFRIEND *admires her* CHOIR: *Stops hum of lament. Silence.*
	…Will you?'

CHOIR: JNR SISTER *is called and lamented by* CHOIR *as she leaves her position on stage, then hummed, underscoring dialogue into next scene.*

Scene Two

A moment as JNR SISTER *leaves.*
CHOIR *underscoring following dialogue with a hummed melody.*

GIRLFRIEND	Askin me – he asked me if I – askin me if I could –
BOYFRIEND	' – able. You are. You / are – able.'
GIRLFRIEND	Thinks he can ask me – thinks he can sweetmouth me with:
BOYFRIEND	'You are – you is – you do – you able – you look you look like – you able to have the ability the capability the capacity – '
GIRLFRIEND	'to what?'
BOYFRIEND	'To…to…'

GIRLFRIEND	He thinks that's going to…?
BOYFRIEND	' – the aptitude. the talent the touch.'
GIRLFRIEND	'The touch?'
BOYFRIEND	'The – you are – you is – you do – you do got – the touch… The sweetness of your touch – '
GIRLFRIEND	'oh God'
BOYFRIEND	'you do – you is – you are – look at you… Look how – look how *sweet* – '
GIRLFRIEND	'*what?*'
BOYFRIEND	'your touch would – could that… / taste.'
MAMA	He asked you if you could cook?
BOYFRIEND	'The calm, the control, the composure you contain – to – '
GIRLFRIEND	'to what?'
BOYFRIEND	'The capabilities you must have to – '
GIRLFRIEND	'to what?'
BOYFRIEND	'to carry out your – '
	CHOIR: *Hummed melody out, sharply.*
MAMA	oh God
BOYFRIEND	'to – cook.'
DAD	I asked you if you / could cook –
MAMA	You knew I could cook –
DAD	can she / cook?
MAMA	which is why you asked me – you knew – he knew –
DAD	she can't cook
MAMA	you knew. Why did you ask? He knew – he knew before he asked – he asked because he did know – Mama ask him –

NANA	why did you ask?
DAD	She looked like she could eat –
	GRANDDAD *is amused.*
MAMA	*that's* your father.
DAD	A well-fed woman. *That's* my wife.
NANA	*My* daughter –
GRANDDAD	our well-fed daughter.
DAD	But can she cook?
	GIRLFRIEND *says nothing.*
	She doesn't cook.
MAMA	I coached her to cook. Coached them to…
GIRLFRIEND	Why would I cook?
DAD	Why doesn't she cook?
GIRLFRIEND	Mama cooks… Mama cooks, what I eat.
MAMA	They learnt their cooking capabilities from me.
NANA	*I* coached you to cook –
MAMA	I –
NANA	I did. I was the cooker – you was the cookless –
GRANDDAD	you couldn't cook.
GIRLFRIEND	Nana couldn't cook?
DAD	Your mother couldn't cook?
MAMA	Course she could cook –
NANA	– I couldn't cook?
MAMA	Mama could cook
NANA	I couldn't cook?
MAMA	Course she could cook – she coached me – and he knows it

GRANDDAD	you couldn't cook either.
GIRLFRIEND	
GRANDDAD	I coached her. I coached her too. *That's* your… She was a bad learner.
NANA	…Don't mind him. Don't pay him no mind.
MAMA NANA MAMA	
GIRLFRIEND	He asked me if I could cook, Mama –
GRANDDAD	he asked *her* – if she could *cook*?
	GRANDDAD *is amused*.
MAMA	This is how they start –
NANA	oh.
DAD	Have to start somewhere
MAMA	oh.
	GRANDDAD *laughs*.
	This is how your father started with me.
NANA	This is how your father started with me.
MAMA	This is how your father flirted with me. This is how your father's flirting started with me
DAD	still working out where to start with you
MAMA	*eh?*
	GRANDDAD *is amused*.
NANA	He looked like he needed a meal. You looked like you needed a meal.
DAD	I needed a meal.
GRANDDAD	He looked like I did.
NANA	You needed more than a meal

DAD	she looked well-fed.
GRANDDAD	Got more than a meal –
MAMA	eh – what?
GRANDDAD	Got more than I asked.
	DAD *is amused.*
	Got more than –
NANA	don't mind him – don't pay your grandfather no…
GRANDDAD	"I don't know what I'm sayin"
NANA	He don't know what he's / rememberin.
GRANDDAD	"I don't know what I'm rememberin".
	CHOIR: *Hummed melody of lament underscores the following:*
GIRLFRIEND	I'm sayin – 'do I look like someone who can't?'
BOYFRIEND	'You look like – you look like someone who could – '
GIRLFRIEND	'do I look like someone who / couldn't?'
BOYFRIEND	'You look like someone who should.'
GIRLFRIEND	'I know I don't look like someone who / wouldn't – '
BOYFRIEND	'You look like someone who would…'
MAMA	Oh God
BOYFRIEND	' – cook. Who is able… who has the talent…'
	DAD *is amused.*
DAD	He has the / mouth.
NANA	He has the mouth.
MAMA	You had the mouth
DAD	I was better.
GIRLFRIEND	Were you?

DAD	Still am.
GRANDDAD	I was better.
NANA	Oh God. Don't mind / him.
GRANDDAD	I was something
NANA	he thought he was / something.
GRANDDAD	still am something
NANA	still thinks he's something
GRANDDAD	she knows exactly what kinda / something –
NANA	don't mind him –
GRANDDAD	forgotten nothing
NANA	forgotten everything
GRANDDAD	and neither have you.
GRANDDAD NANA	
MAMA	Don't mind them.
BOYFRIEND	'The – '
GIRLFRIEND	'what?'
BOYFRIEND	'The – '
NANA	what did he say?
BOYFRIEND	'The – what can I say… The what is there to say? The what is there to say about you?'
MAMA	Oh God. Mouth.
BOYFRIEND	'The – what is there to say about you?'
DAD	Mouth.
BOYFRIEND	'The what is there left to say about you…?' CHOIR: *Humming of lament out. Silence.* …Will you?'

CHOIR: BOYFRIEND *and* GIRLFRIEND
are called and lamented by CHOIR *as they
leave their positions.*

Scene Three

BOYFRIEND *and* GIRLFRIEND *leave.*
Scene starts with cast dialogue only, CHOIR *silent.*

MAMA	He asked her if she could cook. Oh God.
DAD	I asked you if you could / cook –
MAMA	You knew I could / cook –
DAD	could she cook?
MAMA	Which is why you asked me – you knew – he knew –
DAD	she couldn't cook.
MAMA	You knew. Why did you ask? He knew – you knew before he asked – he asked because he did know – Mama ask / him –
NANA	Why did you ask?
DAD	She looked like she could eat.
	GRANDDAD *is amused.*
MAMA	*That's* their father.
DAD	A well-fed woman. *That's* my / wife.
NANA	*My* daughter –
GRANDDAD	our well-fed daughter.
DAD	Could she cook? She didn't / cook.
MAMA	I coached her to cook. Coached them / to cook.

DAD	Why didn't she cook?
MAMA	They learnt their capabilities / from me.
NANA	*I* coached you to cook – I did. I was the cooker – I was the cooker who coached the cookless. I coached you to / cook –
GRANDDAD	You couldn't cook.
DAD	Your mother couldn't / cook?
MAMA	Course she could cook –
NANA	I couldn't cook?
MAMA	Mama could / cook
NANA	I couldn't cook?
MAMA	Dada, Mama could cook. Course she could cook – she coached me – and he knows / it.
GRANDDAD	You couldn't cook either. I coached her. I coached you too…
MAMA	
GRANDDAD	She was a bad learner.
NANA	Don't mind him. Don't pay him no mind.
MAMA NANA MAMA	
	CHOIR: *Solo female voice of* CHOIR *hums a lament melody underscoring the following dialogue:*
GRANDDAD	He asked her if she could cook.
MAMA	…This is how they start –
NANA	oh.
DAD	Have to start somewhere
MAMA	oh. This is how you started with me.
NANA	This is how your father started with me.

MAMA	This is how you flirted with – (me). This is how your flirting started / with me.
DAD	Still working out where to start with you
MAMA	*eh?*
NANA	He looked like he needed a meal. You looked like you needed a meal.
DAD	I needed a / meal.
GRANDDAD	He looked like I did.
NANA	You needed more than a meal
DAD	she looked well-fed.
GRANDDAD	Got more than a meal – got more than / I asked –
NANA	Don't mind him – don't pay your Father no mind –
GRANDDAD	"I don't know what I'm sayin."
NANA	You don't know what you're / rememberin.
GRANDDAD	"I don't know what I'm rememberin."
MAMA	Oh God.
DAD	He had the mouth
NANA	he had the mouth.
MAMA	You had the mouth
DAD	I was better. Still am.
MAMA	
GRANDDAD	I was better.
NANA	Oh God. Don't mind / him.
GRANDDAD	I was something
NANA	he thinks he's / something
GRANDDAD	still am something

NANA	still thinks he's something
GRANDDAD	she knows exactly what kinda / something –
NANA	don't mind him –
GRANDDAD	forgotten nothing
NANA	forgotten everything
GRANDDAD	and neither have you.
NANA	
GRANDDAD	
	CHOIR: *Lament out.*
MAMA	Don't mind them.
DAD	This thing.
NANA	What did he say?
DAD	I miss them.
NANA	What did he say?
MAMA	Oh God. Mouth.
DAD	Mouth.

CHOIR: DAD *is called and lamented by the* CHOIR *as he leaves his position.*
The hummed lament kicks back in.

Scene Four

A moment as DAD *leaves.*
CHOIR: *Hummed lament underscores the following:*

MAMA   He asked her if she could cook?
Oh God.
He knew I could cook – which is why he
asked me – he knew – that's why he asked –
Mama asked him why he asked – Mama
asked him… That's why he asked.

	CHOIR: *Lament out.*
NANA	
MAMA	
MAMA	*That* was their father… …I coached her to cook. Coached them to cook. They learnt their cooking capabilities / from me.
NANA	I coached you to cook –
MAMA	I –
NANA	I did. I was the cooker – you was the cookless – I was the cooker who coached the cookless… I coached you to cook… You were a / bad learner –
GRANDDAD	You couldn't cook
MAMA	course she / could cook –
NANA	I couldn't cook?
MAMA	Mama could / cook
NANA	I couldn't cook?
MAMA	Dada… Mama could cook. She coached me… and you / know it –
GRANDDAD	You couldn't cook either. I coached her. I coached her too. That's your mother.
MAMA	
GRANDDAD	She was a / bad learner.
NANA	Don't mind him. Don't pay him no… (mind.)
MAMA	
NANA	
MAMA	
	CHOIR: *Lament in, underscoring the following:*
GRANDDAD	He asked her if she could cook.

MAMA	That's how they started –
NANA	oh.
MAMA	This is how he started with me.
NANA	This is how your father started with me.
MAMA	This is how he flirted with me. This is how his flirting / started with me.
NANA	He looked like he needed a meal. You looked like you needed / a meal.
GRANDDAD	He looked like I / did.
NANA	You needed more than a meal. I fed her well.
GRANDDAD	Got more than a meal –
MAMA	eh – what?
GRANDDAD	Got more than / I asked.
NANA	Don't pay your father no mind… he doesn't know / what he's…
GRANDDAD	I don't know what I'm sayin… I don't know what I'm rememberin…
MAMA	Oh God.
NANA	He had the mouth.
MAMA	He had the mouth. He was good.
NANA	Oh God.
GRANDDAD	I was / something
NANA	Don't mind him.
GRANDDAD	…Still am something.
NANA	Still thinks he's / something
GRANDDAD	She knows exactly what kinda something – forgotten nothing
NANA	forgotten everything
GRANDDAD	…And neither have you.

NANA
GRANDDAD

           CHOIR: *Lament out.*

NANA   This thing.

MAMA   Don't mind me.

NANA   This big dying thing.

GRANDDAD   What did she say?

MAMA   I miss them.

NANA   What did she say?

MAMA   Oh God.
                    Mouth.

           CHOIR: MAMA *is called and lamented by* CHOIR *as she leaves her position.*

Scene Five

A moment as MAMA *leaves.*
The CHOIR *is silent.*

NANA   *I* coached her to cook – I did… I was the cooker – she was the cookless – I was the cooker who coached the cookless… I… coached her to (cook)… She was a bad learner.

           Beat

GRANDDAD   You couldn't cook.

NANA   I couldn't cook?
                    I couldn't cook.

GRANDDAD   She couldn't (cook) either…
                    …I coached her. I coached her too.
                    That's our – was our… she was our…
                    She was a bad learner.

NANA	
GRANDDAD	
NANA	Don't pay it no mind. She didn't pay you no… (mind)
GRANDDAD	
NANA	
NANA	He asked her if she could cook. Oh. …This is how you started with me.
	You looked like you needed / a meal.
GRANDDAD	I needed a meal.
	Beat.
NANA	You needed more than / a meal.
GRANDDAD	Got more than a meal.
NANA	
GRANDDAD	Got more than I asked. Got more than…
	Thank you.
NANA	
NANA	Do you know what you're saying?
GRANDDAD	
GRANDDAD	…I know what I'm saying… And I remember.
NANA	He had the mouth.
GRANDDAD	Was I better?
NANA	Oh God.
GRANDDAD	I was something.
NANA	I think you're something.
GRANDDAD	Still am something.
NANA	You are.

GRANDDAD   Forgotten nothing.

NANA

GRANDDAD   …No.
            And neither have you.

NANA
GRANDDAD

GRANDDAD   This thing. This dying thing… This unease.
            This dis-ease.

NANA   I miss them.

NANA
GRANDDAD

GRANDDAD   …What did he say?

            What did he say?

NANA

            Both looking for those that have gone.

            Oh God.
            Oh God.

            Oh God.

            End.

stoning mary

for sam and luke

thanks to ruth little, caryl and maria

stoning mary was first performed at the Royal Court Theatre Downstairs, London, on 1 April 2005. The cast was as follows:

WIFE	Emily Joyce
WIFE EGO/OLDER SISTER EGO	Heather Craney
HUSBAND	Peter Sullivan
HUSBAND EGO/BOYFRIEND EGO	Martin Marquez
MUM	Ruth Sheen
DAD	Alan Williams
CHILD SOLDIER	Cole Edwards
OLDER SISTER	Claire Rushbrook
YOUNGER SISTER	Claire-Louise Cordwell
BOYFRIEND	Rick Warden
CORRECTIONS OFFICER	Gary Dunnington
Director	Marianne Elliott
Designer	Ultz
Lighting Designer	Nigel Edwards
Sound Designer	Ian Dickinson

Characters

WIFE
WIFE EGO
HUSBAND
HUSBAND EGO
MUM
DAD
CHILD SOLDIER (SON), *his hair shaved down to a number one*
OLDER SISTER
YOUNGER SISTER (MARY)
CORRECTIONS OFFICER
BOYFRIEND
BOYFRIEND EGO
OLDER SISTER EGO

The play is set in the country it is performed in.

All characters are white.

All characters start onstage.

Scene titles to be shown.

Names without dialogue indicate active silences between those characters.

/ marks where dialogue starts to overlap.

During 'The Prescription', two actors play each character simultaneously.

One

'The AIDS Genocide. The Prescription.'

WIFE	'If you'd putcha hands – put your hands on me –
	If you'd put your hands on me then you'd know – '
WIFE EGO	said.
WIFE	'Put your hands on me to know'
WIFE EGO	said
WIFE	'handle me to know'
WIFE EGO	I said
WIFE	'handle me. Handle me – handle me – go on.'
	WIFE *shows her shaking hands*.
	'Go on.
	Go on. See… can't. Putcha hands on / me'
WIFE EGO	he gives it –
HUSBAND	'no.'
WIFE	'Putcha' –
HUSBAND	'no.'
WIFE	'Go on' –
WIFE EGO	says –
HUSBAND	'I know.'

WIFE EGO	Says –
HUSBAND	'I know how to handle'
WIFE EGO	says
HUSBAND	'I know how to handle you. Know how to handle you to know – '
WIFE EGO	asks me –
HUSBAND	'why don'tchu put your hands on me?'
WIFE EGO	Says –
HUSBAND	'why don'tchu put your hands on me then?'
HUSBAND EGO	Eyes to the skies it.
HUSBAND	'Go on, put your hands on me – '
HUSBAND EGO	she eyes to the skies it – focus on the floors it
HUSBAND	'what if I want you to that – or you don't want me to get from you what you want from me…? Put me hands on meself if I wanna feel that. Can get me to feel me to feel that can't I? Or you sayin your shakes is somethin special?'
WIFE EGO	Shows me his hands
HUSBAND	'Anyone can do nervous.'
HUSBAND EGO	Hands in pocket
HUSBAND	'Anyone can do nervous well.'
WIFE EGO	Hands in pockets then –
HUSBAND	'Anyone can play nervous well better'n you'
WIFE EGO	hands in pockets doing defiant – doin defiant badly.

HUSBAND EGO	Why would I wanna put my hands anywhere else?
HUSBAND	'Why would I wanna put my hands on anyone else?
	Why would I wanna put my hands on / you?'
WIFE	'You wouldn't know.'
WIFE EGO	Face off the floor – look him in the eye.
HUSBAND EGO	Looks me in the eye now, now she thinks she got somethin to say
WIFE	'You wouldn't know iss been that long'
HUSBAND	'not long enough'
WIFE	'not long enough – never was'
HUSBAND EGO	liar
WIFE	'was it?'
WIFE EGO	Liar
HUSBAND	'I wouldn't know? Wouldn't wanna know.'
WIFE	'You never did know – did know how, didja... husband?'
HUSBAND	'Didn't I?'
WIFE	'Dontcha.'
HUSBAND	'Put me hands on you to the point you didn't know what to do with yourself didja?... Didja. Wife.'
WIFE	
HUSBAND	
WIFE	'Didn't you think it would be like this?

	' "Till death do us" an' all that – y'didn't think it would be like this didja? Didn't think we'd get to this. Didn't think we'd be doin this. Didn't think we'd get to this part. Y'didn't think dyin would draw out so dramatic, didja?'
WIFE EGO	Eyes to the skies it.
	He eyes to the skies it, buyin a breather.
HUSBAND	'Blinked and missed the good bits did I?'
WIFE	'What?'
HUSBAND	'Nuthin.'
WIFE	'What?'
HUSBAND	'Blinked and / missed the – '
WIFE	'Huh?'
HUSBAND	'Nuthin.'
WIFE EGO	Waitin on me to 'what' it again, wantin me to 'what' it again to get his attention –
HUSBAND	
WIFE EGO	but I won't.
WIFE	'You got nuthin to say?'
HUSBAND EGO	
WIFE EGO	He says nothing.
WIFE	'You got nothing to say then?'
HUSBAND	
WIFE EGO	Can't say nuthin
WIFE	'You got nothin to say to me – and don't be lookin away – '
HUSBAND	'what?'

WIFE EGO	I said –
WIFE	'don't be looking – you're doing that – '
HUSBAND	'I'm looking / atcha.'
WIFE	'That thing.'
WIFE EGO	Eyes to the side like I won't notice.
WIFE	'That thing that – '
HUSBAND EGO	eyes to the side – she won't notice.
HUSBAND	'I'm lookin atcha'
WIFE EGO	lookin thru me now like I won't notice that neither
WIFE	'that winds me up – '
HUSBAND	'I'm lookin / atcha – '
WIFE	'that winds me up – you know – you're not – that thing thatcha do – do it on / purpose'
HUSBAND	'I'm lookin – '
WIFE	'do it on purpose to piss me off – '
HUSBAND	'Pissed off are ya? Pissed off are ya?'
WIFE	'Piss me off think you're smart'
HUSBAND	'Just you is it? Pissed off are ya?'
WIFE	'This you fightin?'
HUSBAND	'This ain't fightin.'
WIFE	'This ain't fightin…? This is you "not fightin for it" is it…?
	This is you "not wantin to" is it? This is you not "puttin out" over that prescription is it?
	…Oh.'

HUSBAND	
	Beat.
HUSBAND	'Stand still.'
HUSBAND EGO	She says nuthin then.
WIFE EGO	I got nuthin good to say.
HUSBAND	'Stand still will yer.'
WIFE EGO	Got nuthin good I can be bothered to say.
HUSBAND	'And y'look fine'
HUSBAND EGO	liar
WIFE EGO	he says.
HUSBAND	'Y'look well.'
HUSBAND EGO	Liar.
WIFE EGO	Gives it that.
WIFE	'You stand still.'
WIFE EGO	Think
WIFE	you look better'n I do
WIFE EGO	say
WIFE	'Y'lookin better'n – '
WIFE EGO	lies.
HUSBAND	'No I don't.'
WIFE EGO	
HUSBAND EGO	Clocks me then, then looks away.
WIFE EGO	Hands out the pockets, fraid to be free, fingers on the restless, hands on the shake-down back in again, balled.
WIFE	Show me your hands.
	'Show me your hands – '

HUSBAND	'show me your hands'
WIFE	'you show me yourn first.'
HUSBAND	
HUSBAND	
HUSBAND EGO	This all part a it?
WIFE	'You nervous a me…? Are ya… are yer?'
HUSBAND	
WIFE	
WIFE	'You are ain'tcha.'
HUSBAND	'You ain't what I gotta be nervous of.'
WIFE	'You are ain'tcha, ain'tcha?'
HUSBAND	'What you got I gotta be nervous of? What you got – I already got it.'
WIFE	'I already got it.'
HUSBAND	'Got it from you.'
WIFE	'I got it from you.'
HUSBAND	
WIFE	
HUSBAND	'You nervous a that?'
HUSBAND EGO	Eyes on the prescription.
WIFE EGO	Eyes away. Embarrassed.
HUSBAND EGO	Eyes to the floor like there's summat there of interest
WIFE EGO	little on the look away
HUSBAND EGO	she ain't sure where – but away from –
HUSBAND	'What you scared of? What *you* scared of then?'

WIFE	'Not you, for a start.'
HUSBAND	'No?'
WIFE	'No.'
HUSBAND	'… No.
	That?' (*The prescription.*)
WIFE	'No.'
HUSBAND	'No? You sure? You sure? Sure are yer? Are yer?'
HUSBAND EGO	Cos she doesn't –
WIFE EGO	stop shaking.

Two

'The Child Soldier.'

MUM *and* DAD *are trying to think.*

MUM	Umm.
	Umm…
DAD	Er.
MUM	Umm.
	DAD *coughs.*
	Yes?
DAD	Er…
MUM	Yes?
DAD	Um… you?
MUM	Nothing.

DAD	Nothing?
MUM	…Nothing.
	…I can't think of nothing good…

Three

'The AIDS Genocide. The Prescription.'

HUSBAND

WIFE

WIFE

HUSBAND EGO	Clock it –
WIFE EGO	glance –
HUSBAND EGO	she givin it –
WIFE EGO	glance –
HUSBAND EGO	she givin it, 'fraid to give the prescription the good long look.
WIFE EGO	Eyes to the skies it
HUSBAND EGO	the good long look
WIFE EGO	he eyes to the skies it like how he does –
HUSBAND EGO	the good long look I want to but won't.
WIFE EGO	Like somethin up there's gonna save you.
	WIFE EGO *laughs*.
	Like someone up there's gonna save you.

HUSBAND

WIFE

WIFE EGO	Like some higher bein's gonna bother bein here – to save your arse… or mine.
WIFE	'Virgin Mary ain't watchin no more and bet baby Jesus is bored.'
HUSBAND	'What?'
WIFE	'Virgin – '
HUSBAND	'*what*?'
WIFE	'Nuthin.'
HUSBAND	'What?'
WIFE	'It ain't like – '
HUSBAND	'huh?'
WIFE	'It ain't like – it ain't like – '
HUSBAND	'what?'
WIFE EGO	Said
WIFE	'it ain't like I'm becomin critical a your capabilities or somethin – it ain't that, I wouldn't do that. Would I? Husband.'
WIFE EGO	Said.
WIFE	'And I ain't makin a meal over no… manhoodness. Or manhood. Your manhood.'
HUSBAND EGO	What?
WIFE EGO	It ain't that –
HUSBAND EGO	*what*?
WIFE EGO	It ain't that
WIFE	'It ain't that, I wouldn't do that neither. Would I? Would I? Am I?'

WIFE EGO	Said
WIFE	'And I ain't produced the part about providing – '
HUSBAND	'it ain't about that – '
WIFE	'it ain't about that – '
WIFE EGO	said.
WIFE	'It ain't about that, no. Ain't got nuthin to do with the practicalities of what you can provide is it?
	…That we can afford one, when what we need is two…
	That we got – one – when what we need is… two.
	That one prescription for life – '
WIFE EGO	for a life
WIFE	'isn't enough for…'
	WIFE EGO *shows two fingers*.
	'Is it… Now I ain't brought that up.'
WIFE EGO	
HUSBAND EGO	
WIFE	'Cos I ain't standin here sayin it's me insteada you – am I?
	Ain't here sayin me over you am I?
	Not here sayin all the reasons why it shouldn't be you, am I?
	"Should be me. Should be me."
	Not sayin that – not doin that.
	Am I that? Am I sayin it's that? I wouldn't bring that up and say that either would I? Am I sayin that? Like that? No. I / ain't.'
HUSBAND	'It's not about / that.'

WIFE	'Not about that, no. We're not – '
HUSBAND	'fightin – '
WIFE	'like that – are we. No. No, we're not… '
HUSBAND	
WIFE	
WIFE	'…But it is you who can't make a course a meds without messin it up – tabs left in the bottle – medicine left in the jar – lets one bout a somethin simple knock you back a week dunno what to do with yourself.'
HUSBAND	'I liked you lookin after me.'
WIFE`	'You had to be looked after.'
HUSBAND	'You liked lookin after me'
WIFE	'you had to be looked after.'
HUSBAND	'I letchu'
WIFE	'you weren't in no position to not.'
HUSBAND	'In sickness and in health and all / that'
WIFE	'A chill.'
HUSBAND	'A head cold.'
WIFE	'A head cold.'
HUSBAND	'A heavy cold.'
WIFE	'A heavy cold then.'
HUSBAND	'Flu.'
WIFE	'Y'had a chill.
	When have you ever looked after me…?'
HUSBAND	

WIFE	'When have you (ever) – you wouldn't know / how'
HUSBAND	'You're never sick.'
WIFE	'You'd get confused lookin after anyone who weren't you, you would.'
HUSBAND	'You're never / sick – '
WIFE	'You wouldn't know if I was.'
HUSBAND	'You haven't been.'
WIFE	'Till now.'
HUSBAND EGO	Not a shake about her shit now.
HUSBAND	'Thought you was fuckin nervous?'
HUSBAND EGO	Not a shake about / her shit now.
WIFE	'Thought you had somethin to say.'
HUSBAND EGO	Rock solid.
HUSBAND	'Thought you was playin it all that?'
HUSBAND EGO	Not a shake not a tremble –
HUSBAND	'putchur hands on me see how scared I am'
WIFE EGO	no, don't.
HUSBAND EGO	Steady as fuck – mumblin –
WIFE	'no.'
HUSBAND	'What?'
WIFE EGO	Don't.
WIFE	'Like you never heard'
HUSBAND	'like I'm meant to hear'
WIFE	'what.'
HUSBAND	'What?'

WIFE	'No.'
HUSBAND EGO	Won't speak up. She. Won't respond. Me.
HUSBAND	
HUSBAND EGO	Looks away embarrassed. Looks away from it embarrassed – look at her.
HUSBAND	
WIFE	
HUSBAND EGO	Eyes to the floorin it like I've done her somethin.
	Playin powerless
WIFE EGO	play powerless
HUSBAND EGO	playin powerless badly.
WIFE	'What if I wanna look after you?'
HUSBAND	'What if I wanna live lookin after you?
	(I'd) look after you and love it.'
WIFE EGO	Liar.
HUSBAND EGO	Liar.
	Somethin down there? Somethin down there to help her with her sulk? Helpin her with her shameless?
	HUSBAND *runs his fingers through his hair.*
	WIFE *watches him.*
WIFE EGO	Usedta be my job. Usually my job, loved me doin it –
WIFE	'love doin it'
HUSBAND	'what?'
WIFE EGO	Fingers thru his follicles... lovely.

HUSBAND EGO	Finish with a fistful of hair. Never used to do this
HUSBAND	'never used to lose this'
WIFE	'what?'
HUSBAND	
WIFE	
HUSBAND EGO	Old.
HUSBAND	
HUSBAND	'Older.'
WIFE EGO	Sad.
WIFE	'Sadder.'
HUSBAND	'What?'
WIFE	'Nuthin.'
HUSBAND EGO	Sick.
WIFE EGO	Sicker.
HUSBAND EGO	Eyes on the lookaway – won't meet mine.
WIFE EGO	Anywhere else – but his.
HUSBAND EGO	Eyes to the skies it like how I do.
WIFE EGO	'Fraid to give it (*Re: the prescription*.) the good long look I want to.
HUSBAND	'We fightin?'
WIFE	
HUSBAND	'Feels like fightin.'
WIFE	'This ain't fightin.'
HUSBAND	'We fightin yet?'
WIFE	'…No.'

HUSBAND	'You finished yet?'
WIFE	'No.'
HUSBAND	'You bored yet?'
WIFE	'…No.'
HUSBAND EGO	Eyes to the skies it like somethin up there's gonna save her like some higher bein would bother bein here
HUSBAND	'God got bored before we did.'
WIFE	'What?'
HUSBAND EGO	Like some higher bein would bother botherin with us.

Four

'The Child Soldier.'

MUM *and* DAD *are trying to think.*

MUM	Umm.
	Umm…
DAD	Er.
MUM	Umm…
	DAD *coughs.*
	Yes?
DAD	Er…
MUM	Yes?
DAD	Um.
MUM	…To watch… to watch him. Lovin that. Lovin doin that. Doing that.

Er.

Hold.
To hold him – his hands his fingers –
fingertips, on to him, on to his gaze – into
his gaze his any-little-bit-a-him, to hold
that – on to that – to have that, into that,
to have and to hold that. To have that to
hold…

Having that to hold on to.
Having that.
Doing that.
Miss that.

…To smell. Have his smell. Smell his
smell, smell his smell on him – smell his
smell on me. The never-get-used-to-that,
the never-get-enough-of-that – the after-
bath aroma, the first thing of a mornin –
the just-come-in-from-out wanting more
of that smell. The smell – lovin that the
smell of lovin that – lovin smellin that.
Me doin that.
Waiting for that.
That smell.
That.
His. Him.
Doin that.
Me.
Miss it.

Umm…

Touch.
Touch him. Doin that –

DAD	said that.
MUM	I said –
DAD	you said that / already

MUM   I said / that?

DAD   You did.

MUM   'To hold,' I said, '*to hold*'

DAD   touch – hold / whatever –

MUM   I'm sayin it again then

DAD   you said – you said – just sayin you said /
                  it already

MUM   to 'touch' him – if that's alright with /
                  you –

DAD   nuthin to do with / me –

MUM   nah it never was.

DAD

MUM

MUM   To kiss him –

DAD   he hated bein kissed

MUM   by you – to kiss / him

DAD   he hated bein kissed.

MUM   By. You. Hated you trying.

                  To kiss him – here… here.

                  Catch him off when he weren't watching,
                  land one on him when he weren't ready.

MUM	DAD
Catch him off with a quick –	To watch – to watch him.
catch him off when I was.	Watch how he'd watch.
Catch him off just because.	Watch how he'd watch
Catch him with a kiss to	back. Watch how he'd
comfort.	watch me back.

DAD   Watch your back while he's watching
                  you.

Watch yourself while he's watching.
There's that.
There was that.
Hold. To hold him. To hold on to him.
Hold. Touch.
To hold him down.
Pin him down.
Pin him down, play pin him down, play
down, play hard, play dead. Play till he
pinned me, till he would pin me – till he
would pin me to the point of playin for
real. To the point of playin till there was
no point – to the point of not playin –
pinning each other down to prove a point.
…There's that.
There's 'playin' that.
Having to play that.
There is (that)…

Beat.

Umm…

MUM	To smell.
DAD	He smelt of you.
MUM	He smelt of / him –
DAD	he smelt of you.
MUM	He smelt / like –
DAD	He did – he smelt of you – there was no smell of him – there was no smell of him left – he had no smell of his own the only aroma around him was – the only smell left on him was – the only linger left on him was *yourn* – was from *you*.

The smell of whatever you smothered
yourself with – of whatever you drowned
yourself in.

Whatever you drowned yourself in he
was drownin right there in the
disgustingness of it with yer.
The smell of your not-quite-right.
The smell of the didn't-cost-much.
The smell of the two-for-one.
The smell a the been-on-a-bit-too-long –

MUM   you / wouldn't

DAD   the smell a the nuthin-natural-about-it, the
nuthin-nice-about-it. He smelt like that –

MUM   you wouldn't / know –

DAD   he smelled like that he smelt like you
smell – how you still smell – he smelt of
/ you.

MUM   You wouldn't know.

DAD   I wouldn't know what he smelt like?

MUM   You wouldn't know what he / smelt like –

DAD   I dunno what anythin smells like.

MUM   You wouldn't know what he smelled like
you didn't get close / enough

DAD   I don't know what anythin smells like
when you're around

MUM   he wouldn't letchu get close enough to
know – you don't get close enough to
anything to smell / anything –

DAD   when you're around the smell of anythin
else – everything else gets obliterated by
your spray-it-as-you-feel-it-full-on
artificial / stink.

MUM   You don't get that close and you
wouldn't know what he smelled like cos
he never letchu get close enough to / him.

DAD	Stinkin out the place – I dunno what you smell like
MUM	I don't want you to smell me.
DAD	You dunno whatchu smell like
MUM	why would I wanna smell myself?
	Why would I wanna smell myself?
DAD	(If) you did you wouldn't / ask –
MUM	Like some kinda dog…
DAD	
MUM	Don't think so. Don't think so – and I don't wantchu near –
DAD	catch the smell a the natural you, drop down dead a / shock.
MUM	Don'tchu come near – don'tchu come nearer –
DAD	genetically modified mothafuckin – you're like that you are, you are – you're like them monster seeds spreadin their monster selves outta their monster labs over the happily growin natural shit that was already there, happy growin in the field –
MUM	don'tchu come / nearer
DAD	you're like that you are.
MUM	Stay / there –
DAD	Contaminate – contamination. Contaminate everything you come into contact with, with your / stink –
MUM	I mean it
DAD	genetically modified contaminated fuck contaminating naturally organic me / and he –

MUM   you never got close enough to him to
             know – you wouldn't know how –

DAD   I wouldn't know / how?

MUM   he never letchu near.

             Beat.

DAD   You're never naked of someone else's
             bottled version of someone else you are –
             always sprayed up sprayed on – sprayed
             on ya thick and thorough, spray it on
             thick and thorough enough might just
             lose the real you for good – I never get
             close enough?

MUM   You never get / close enough.

DAD   I never get close enough do I?

MUM   Stay there –

DAD   I never get close –

MUM   don'tchu come – you never wanted to –

DAD   you want me to?

MUM   You never wanted to.

DAD   You want me to? You want me to – you
             want me close?

MUM

DAD   You want me to now? Do yer? You want
             me now…?

MUM

DAD

MUM

             MUM *nods. Just.*

DAD

MUM	
MUM	
DAD	…Nah. Still don't want you do I?
	Still don't wanna do yer do I?
	Beat.
	His laugh.
MUM	
DAD	His laugh.
MUM	…He didn't / laugh.
DAD	His laughter. Me and he's laughter. He laughed with me.
MUM	
DAD	Our, more-than-a-smile-or-a-smirk, that we shared –
MUM	
DAD	that you never knew nuthin about.
MUM	You don't laugh.
DAD	Our head back, eyes streamin, free, full, frank, full-on – laughter. Laughin hard – laughin long – laughin loud like that… Over you. Having that. Doing / that.
MUM	His time.
DAD	Doin / that.
MUM	His time he'd / spend.
DAD	Laughin like that
MUM	his time he'd spend with me –

DAD	laughing at you like that
MUM	the time he'd make to / spend with me
DAD	laughin at your *smell*.
MUM	The time he did spend with me.
DAD	Laughin at y'you and your smell, with me, like that. We did. That. Doin that. Miss that. Miss that of him. I do.
MUM	
MUM	
DAD	
MUM	I wear it cos he bought it.
DAD	He bought it for a joke.
MUM	
DAD	
MUM	I wear it because he liked it.
DAD	He liked it for a joke.
MUM	…It reminds me of / him.
DAD	You are a joke.
	Beat.
MUM	If you were gone –
DAD	I'm not gone tho
MUM	if you were / gone –
DAD	but I'm not the one who's gone / tho.
MUM	if you were gone there'd be nuthin to remind me of you

DAD	I wouldn't wantchu to remember / me
MUM	there's nuthin good to / remember
DAD	I wouldn't want to be remembered.
MUM	Good then.
DAD	Good.
MUM	Good.
DAD	Good.
MUM	*Good.*
	Beat.
DAD	Not by you.

Five

'The Prescription.'

HUSBAND	'I'm not fightin for it'
WIFE EGO	leans back body language denyin his lie.
HUSBAND EGO	She on the front foot for effect.
WIFE	'I'm not gonna act like I won't.'
	Beat.
HUSBAND	'But I am fitter'
WIFE EGO	laid it back like it ent fightin talk
WIFE	'I'm younger.'
HUSBAND	'But I'm stronger.'
HUSBAND EGO	She on the metaphorical lookaway
WIFE	'but I'm smart–'

WIFE EGO	he eyes to the skies it
WIFE	'–ter. I'm smarter. I am.'
HUSBAND	'I earn more – '
WIFE	'not enough to cover two'
HUSBAND	'more'n we need for one.'
WIFE	'What – so the other can watch the other stay well in comfort?'
WIFE EGO	Stung an' on the step back. Nice. Watch – hand out to the side – watch, watch – reachin for the chair –
WIFE	'or enough for a hot hired-in home help?'
HUSBAND EGO	Lean on the chair back
WIFE EGO	think he's gonna fling it –
HUSBAND EGO	she's on the flinch and I don't know why
WIFE EGO	sits instead.
HUSBAND EGO	Sit at her front. Sit at the front of it, sit at her fuckin front of it.
WIFE EGO	He on the lean forward
HUSBAND EGO	she on the step back.
HUSBAND	'You scared a somethin?'
HUSBAND EGO	She eyes away it.
WIFE EGO	Doin the dance that we do.
WIFE	'What I gotta be scared of?'
HUSBAND	It's me who's scared a you
WIFE	what?
WIFE EGO	Mumblin – mumblin –
WIFE	'what?'

HUSBAND	It's me who's –
WIFE	'what?'
HUSBAND	'It's me who's scared a you.'
WIFE EGO	He on the lean back.
HUSBAND EGO	She eases forward.
HUSBAND	'I can earn more.'
WIFE	'I can adapt more.'
HUSBAND	'I can work longer – '
WIFE	'I can work nearer.'
WIFE EGO	Eyes to the floor. Eyes to the sky then. He eyes the gods and away from anywhere near me.
WIFE	'Lookin for somethin?'
WIFE EGO	He eyes to the skies stayin / there.
WIFE	'Lookin for something?'
HUSBAND	'I can support the girls – '
WIFE	'this ain't about the girls'
HUSBAND	'I can / support – '
WIFE	'you bringin the girls into this? Don't be bringing our girls / into this.'
HUSBAND	'I can talk to the girls'
WIFE	'our girls don't need talkin to – '
HUSBAND	'I can support / the girls'
H. AND WIFE EGO	fight.
WIFE	'I can raise the girls – '
H. AND WIFE EGO	fight.
HUSBAND	'I can teach the girls'

H. AND WIFE EGO	fight
WIFE	'what?'
HUSBAND	'I can teach the girls – '
WIFE	'exactly *what*?'
H. AND WIFE EGO	*Fight* –
WIFE	'Firstborn don't need teachin and Mary thinks she knows it all.'
HUSBAND	'Where she get that from?'
WIFE	'I wonder.'
HUSBAND	'Do that.'
HUSBAND EGO	Mouth on her like her mother.
HUSBAND	'Mary's like her mother – '
WIFE	'an' Firstborn's like her father – God help / her – '
HUSBAND	'They'll need their father.'
HUSBAND EGO	Me.
WIFE EGO	Fight.
WIFE	'The *girls'll* need their *mother*.'
WIFE EGO	Me.
HUSBAND EGO	Fight.
HUSBAND	'I can protect the girls – '
WIFE	'*I* can protect the / girls – '
HUSBAND	'you don't call this fightin?'
WIFE	'This ain't fightin – '
HUSBAND	'you wouldn't call this / fightin?'
WIFE	'This ain't fightin – '
HUSBAND	'This ain't fightin?'

WIFE	'This ain't fightin – you still standin an' the prescription ain't mine / yet'
HUSBAND	'I'm not gonna make like to fight you / for it – '
WIFE	'I'm not gonna act like I – '

The CHILD SOLDIER *stands with them, with his bloodied machete.*

His head is shaved down to a number one.

HUSBAND *and* WIFE *are both taken by surprise.*

Six

'The Child Soldier.'

DAD	Outta things to say? You run outta good things to say?
	You run outta things to say / about him?
MUM	There's not enough words –
DAD	that you know –
MUM	there's not enough good words –
DAD	that you know –
MUM	not enough good long words out there to say about him – about my son
DAD	*my son*
MUM	not enough of them – so I'll stop.
DAD	Wish you would.

MUM	I'll say nuthin.
DAD	Wish you would.
MUM	There is nothing to say –
DAD	there's plenty to say – there was plenty / to say –
MUM	don't start
DAD	before you –
MUM	don't / start
DAD	lost him –
MUM	*don't*. His hair – his hair – .
DAD	
MUM	His hair. Lovin that. His (hair) – his cut of his hair –
DAD	he had my hair
MUM	he did not
DAD	had my hair / line
MUM	he did not.
DAD	He got his hair from / me
MUM	he did *not*. His cut of how he'd wear his hair… Letting me cut his hair – doing that. Seeing that. Fingers thru that. To see that. Have that. Have that remind me – have that remind me of –
DAD	mine.
MUM	How yourn weren't. How yourn weren't ever quite – able – weren't never quite… was it? Of how

yourn usedta be – how yourn usedta *try*
to be – when you used to *try* to bother –

DAD when there was something worth
bothering about

MUM even then you never got it right – get it
right

DAD when you were worth bothering about

MUM still weren't worth waitin / for –

DAD before I realised there was no point. It
was / pointless.

MUM You still weren't worth waitin for even
then, still / weren't worth that

DAD it was pointless. You were / pointless.

MUM and even when you tried – what you
called 'tried' – what / you passed for
'tried' –

DAD you are pointless and it was pointless /
trying

MUM even that hadda knack a not lookin right.
Never looked right. Always somethin
not-right-lookin about yer.

Beat.

DAD You weren't worth trying over –
y'weren't worth workin that hard over…
Didn't have to work that hard to work
you over –
Did I?

MUM

DAD

MUM His hair looked better'n yourn ever
would –

DAD	in fact you was easy –
MUM	better'n yourn ever / could
DAD	very easy.
MUM	You weren't able.
DAD	Bit of a bike.
MUM	Outshone by our son.
DAD	Somethin of the slag about yer.
MUM	Every time.
DAD	Somethin of the slut –
MUM	*all* the time
DAD	somethin of the *used* about yer.
	Beat.
MUM	To watch –
DAD	you'd watch –
MUM	you'd watch –
DAD	I never.
MUM	You would –
DAD	I never –
MUM	yes you did – you'd watch him – you'd watch him – you watched you did. Watch his hair and wish it was you – watch me wash it and wish it was you –
DAD	I never –
MUM	watch me cuttin it, wishin it was / you –
DAD	I never / lost
MUM	you watched you watched you did – I watched you watchin, I saw yer – pathetic

DAD	I never – (lost him.)
MUM	pitiful.
DAD	I never lost him –
MUM	pitiful. You are –
DAD	did I?
MUM	Pitiful and pathetic hand in hand you / are –
DAD	He weren't with me.
MUM	He was never with you –
DAD	he weren't out with me –
MUM	you never took him out –
DAD	he loved our inside time –
MUM	he loved goin out with me more –
DAD	till you lost him.
MUM	They *took* –
DAD	till you / lost –
MUM	I never lost him – I didn't I didn't I didn't… They took him. They took him. They *took* him.
	They did.
DAD	
MUM	
MUM	
MUM	
DAD	Wash it now…
MUM	
DAD	Run your hands over his number one now.

MUM	
DAD	Put your hands to his head now.
MUM	
DAD	And see where it gets you.

Seven

'The Child Soldier.'

HUSBAND *and* WIFE (*from 'The Prescription'*).

The CHILD SOLDIER *still holds his machete.*

HUSBAND	There's nuthin –
WIFE	there is / nuthin –
HUSBAND	there is nothing –
WIFE	we don't have –
HUSBAND	nothing – we don't / got –
WIFE	if he's lookin for / somethin
HUSBAND	we don't –
WIFE	have it.
HUSBAND	If you're lookin for somethin –
WIFE	if he's lookin for / somethin –
HUSBAND	y'wanna look somewhere else go somewhere / else
WIFE	somewhere / else
HUSBAND	anywhere else
WIFE	for your somethin.

HUSBAND   Cos we've got nuthin here.

WIFE   We don't

HUSBAND   we don't

WIFE   we don't –

HUSBAND   have anything –

WIFE   we / don't –

HUSBAND   for yer. Something ain't here, nuthin ain't here – if somethin was here we'd say if anything was here we'd tell yer –

WIFE   honest.

HUSBAND   Honest – there's –

WIFE   there is / nuthin

HUSBAND   there is nothing –

WIFE   we don't / have

HUSBAND   nuthin here –

WIFE   no. No.

HUSBAND   Anything here.

WIFE   No. No.

HUSBAND   Something here for yer. Honest…

                Honest.

HUSBAND

CHILD

WIFE

CHILD

HUSBAND

WIFE

WIFE   Except – if it's food –

HUSBAND	do you want food?
WIFE	Does he want / food?
HUSBAND	This isn't –
WIFE	is it / food?
HUSBAND	about that.
WIFE	We have that we have that we have that if that's what you want – if that's the somethin you want we have that but apart from / that –
HUSBAND	Apart / from –
WIFE	apart from that
HUSBAND	we don't have nuthin.
WIFE	There is –
HUSBAND	nuthin –
WIFE	there / is
HUSBAND	there is nothin – there is nothin here for you – that we have…
WIFE	No.
	Except food…
HUSBAND	Apart from that –
WIFE	apart from that – no there is –
HUSBAND	nuthin else.
WIFE	No. No.
CHILD	
HUSBAND	
CHILD	
HUSBAND	

WIFE	Except – if it's money
HUSBAND	if you came for money
WIFE	is it money?
HUSBAND	If you came / for that
WIFE	Does he want / money?
HUSBAND	Is this about that?
WIFE	If he needs –
HUSBAND	you want –
WIFE	does he need –
HUSBAND	look d'you / want –
WIFE	some money?
HUSBAND	We don't –
WIFE	is it that?
HUSBAND	We don't / have –
WIFE	Is it that?
HUSBAND	We don't got / any –
WIFE	A bit.
HUSBAND	We don't have –
WIFE	only a bit
HUSBAND	any money. We don't.
WIFE	…Just a bit.

WIFE *digs into* HUSBAND*'s front trouser pockets and pulls out his coins. She shows to the* CHILD SOLDIER. *He doesn't respond.*

…Apart from / that…

HUSBAND	Apart from –

WIFE	apart from that –
HUSBAND	there's nothing…
	There's nothing that we have for you.
WIFE	No. No.
	There is nothing for you here – tell him. Tell him. Tell him that.

Beat.

CHILD	
WIFE	
WIFE	Except my ring.
HUSBAND	…This isn't about –
WIFE	my rings
HUSBAND	it's not about –
WIFE	both my rings
HUSBAND	it's not about that.
	Is it?
WIFE	They come off –
HUSBAND	this is / about
WIFE	I can gettem off –
HUSBAND	this is about somethin –
WIFE	I can get them / off.
HUSBAND	this is about something else.
WIFE	I can I can. I can. If that's what you / want.
HUSBAND	He doesn't / want –
WIFE	if that's what he's here / for –
HUSBAND	he's not here for that

WIFE   If that's what he needs…

                  WIFE *continually tries to twist her rings off. They won't come.*

                  Apart from this –

HUSBAND   this / is –

WIFE   apart from them

HUSBAND   this is / about

WIFE   after that

HUSBAND   this is about us.

WIFE   We have nothing else –

HUSBAND   this is about us.

WIFE   …Will he go?

HUSBAND   Isn't it?

                  Beat.

                  Us not being them.

                  Cos we're not them.

                  Cos there is nuthin / else.

WIFE   No. No. *Tell him…*

HUSBAND   And he's not here for / the –

WIFE   It's not much.

HUSBAND   And he's not come for / the –

WIFE   I know it's not / much –

HUSBAND   he's not here for that

WIFE   but this'll be everything.

HUSBAND   There's nothing

WIFE   there is / nothing

HUSBAND	yes there's nothing –
WIFE	no.
HUSBAND	There is nothing – there's nothing – there is nothing else –
WIFE	no. No.
HUSBAND	There is nothing else we can do…
	Is there. Is there? Is there.
CHILD	
HUSBAND	
CHILD	
HUSBAND	

WIFE *offers up the prescription to the* CHILD SOLDIER.

Beat.

The CHILD SOLDIER *destroys it.*

CHILD	Beg.

Eight

'Stoning Mary.'

YOUNGER SISTER (MARY) *wears heavy glasses.*

CORR. OFFICER   …Mary.

OLDER SISTER

YOUNGER SISTER

OLDER SISTER

OLDER SISTER

OLDER SISTER   Since when you gotta thing with your things?

Since when you gotta thing with your things?

YOUNGER SISTER Huh?

OLDER SISTER   How long since you –

YOUNGER SISTER I dunno

OLDER SISTER   since when didju – ?

YOUNGER SISTER I dunno.

OLDER SISTER   You dunno? You dunno? Y'don't know?

Beat.

…Stressful…

Don't suit yer do they –

YOUNGER SISTER I / dunno

OLDER SISTER   dunno much do yer they don't even suit – they don't – you need 'em?

YOUNGER SISTER I –

OLDER SISTER   Still gotcha hair then. Letchu still got that?

YOUNGER SISTER

OLDER SISTER   S'grown.

YOUNGER SISTER

OLDER SISTER   Make you look older – make you look old – make you look – they do – they don't – someone said they did – whoever said they did was lyin – who in here said that then, four eyes?

YOUNGER SISTER

OLDER SISTER   Huh? Huh?

YOUNGER SISTER No one.

OLDER SISTER They was lyin – make y'look – they do,
make y'look… not like you – not like
you look – not like how you look.
Usedta.
Usedta look.
Before.
Looked before.
Before you haddem you seen yourself,
Sis?

YOUNGER SISTER

OLDER SISTER You seen yourself – you seen yourself in
em?

YOUNGER SISTER …Yeh –

OLDER SISTER no you ain't.
Someone say they look nice…?
Someone say they look alright – yeh?

YOUNGER SISTER No

OLDER SISTER cos they ain't.

Someone say they look the shit? They
was lyin – cos they don't – you think
they look alright?

You think they look alright?

YOUNGER SISTER

OLDER SISTER You think they look alright?

YOUNGER SISTER I –

OLDER SISTER you don't know – you wouldn't know
you wouldn't know you never did know –
cos they don't – they don't – they don't
suit they don't even suit yer and how
long you had a thing with your things
then?

YOUNGER SISTER I / dunno.

OLDER SISTER Don' look good at all do they. Do they.
Do they?

Do they?

Beat.

Nah. No. They do not.

You goin blind – sight shot to shit is / it?

YOUNGER SISTER No.

OLDER SISTER Not no fuckin fashion accessory tho are
they – are they?

Are they?

YOUNGER SISTER

OLDER SISTER Don't think so… No.

Beat.

YOUNGER SISTER No.

OLDER SISTER No. They ain't – you get tested – you
long or short?

YOUNGER SISTER They said –

OLDER SISTER love someone to test my shit – check my
shit – check me out – get me tested –

YOUNGER SISTER they think / I'm –

OLDER SISTER love to – love that. Love to love that. But
no. No chance. Me have that? – I don't
think so. Me have somethin? – I don't
think so. Someone give a fuck – so very
fuckin no. You requess a test or did they
offer – bet they was on the offer – little
freeness for yer – you goin blind or
somethin – look how thick they are – how
thick are they? How thick is them things?

190   debbie tucker green

YOUNGER SISTER I ent goin / blind.

OLDER SISTER *Thick* thick. I could be an' no one would
care no one would give a fuck – I could
be goin blind and no one wouldn't know
– no one wouldn't wanna know – know
to not give a fuck know to do that – know
how to do that – easy – an' they look like
bottle ends look like vases look like they
gone and got a bit happy on the thickness
front – had a ton a glass left over and
stuck 'em on the front a your face – they
look fuckin 'orrible.
Look like you got a problem –
look like you a bit back-a-the-class –
bit on the 'don't knows' –
bit on the retardative, you long or short of
it or what – which is the what / of it?

YOUNGER SISTER When things is / close –

OLDER SISTER Mine could be worse – worse'n yourn –
you lucky.

You know, y'know? You're lucky to
know – I'm here without a whatever
thinkin my what I'm seein is normal
when it might not ain't – when it might
be fallin well short of what it should be –
when I might be more'n half than blind
meself and worse'n yourn ever is.

Beat.

Least you know… at least you know…
y'know?… Love someone to test my
shit… would love that…

YOUNGER SISTER They asked –

OLDER SISTER see –

YOUNGER SISTER offered –

OLDER SISTER   bet they did –

YOUNGER SISTER they –

> OLDER SISTER *shakes out two cigarettes*.

OLDER SISTER   see – what, what – and what? So's yous can see what you're doin better – see yourself doin nuthin in here better'n you did before – see what they're doin to you better'n that – you can see what they gonna do better still – and you ain't one to refuse you ain't one to knock back a bit a freeness is it – is it – what – what?

No you ent – what?… What? You stopped?

YOUNGER SISTER I've –

OLDER SISTER   you on the health kick?

YOUNGER SISTER I've stopped.

OLDER SISTER   You who the one who got me started. You the one who started me down that road is gonna sit there and say to me you stopped – nah – I know you ain't – I know you ain't… I know you *ain't* – I know you ain't gonna sit there and gimme *that*.

Beat.

…Since when?

YOUNGER SISTER I / dunno.

OLDER SISTER   Since before or after you started sportin your additional eyewear – this the new you – this the new (you) – you goin out healthier'n you was ever in – you plannin on doin that and how much things we do?

YOUNGER SISTER I / dunno –

OLDER SISTER   How much things we do together?

YOUNGER SISTER I / dunno.

OLDER SISTER   How much things we – can we – do we
                 got left to do?

YOUNGER SISTER

OLDER SISTER   Yeh. No. You don't know. People that I
                 put on hold – you don't know – dealins to
                 do that I didn't – y'don't (know) – cos
                 I'm dealin with you cos I'm doin that
                 makin that choice – makin *a* choice –
                 which is whatchu want – you don't know
                 'bout that do yer?

                 No you do not.

                 Me, don't say nuthin cos I don't wantchu
                 knowin – don't want the 'ohh iss alright'
                 – don't wantchur 'sorries' – don't
                 wantchu feelin guiltier'n you already are.
                 Don't clock that do yer?

                 Don't think about that?
                 Do yer. Do yer. Do yer?
                 …No you do not.

                 Come in here – what – what? Wanta little
                 spark-up you sayin you've stopped.
                 Come in here – what – when I coulda
                 sparked up out there and you in here say
                 you've stopped.
                 Come in here to share the thing we usedta
                 do and now you sayin you don't cos you
                 on some health-kick or some such shit –
                 you ain't stopped – you ain't stopped.
                 You ent stopped… have yer?

                 No you have (not) – I coulda.
                 I coulda.
                 I coulda I coulda stopped couldn't I?

YOUNGER SISTER   Couldja.

OLDER SISTER   I coulda stopped coulda stopped if I
hadn't started coulda stopped if I hadn't
got started – someone hadn't *got* me
started in the first fuckin place *Sis* –
couldn't I? Couldn't I?

Beat.

Thank you.

…So you ain't in no position to quit. You
don't get the say-so to say you've
stopped. You don't got the right – you
lost the right – you lost that right when
you started me startin – you lost the right
before you lost your rights, right?

Yeh you did –

YOUNGER SISTER   I didn't haveta come thru.

OLDER SISTER   *I* didn't haveta come.

I didn't haveta come.
I didn't have to come did I? Did I. *Did I?*
– No I did not – and I'm fine thanks –
I'm fuckin fine – I'm doin alright –
thanks. Thanks for askin.
I'm bearin up – y'know. Y'know. You
know?
Not.

YOUNGER SISTER

OLDER SISTER   Huh?

YOUNGER SISTER

OLDER SISTER   *Yeh. Stressful.*

YOUNGER SISTER   I –

OLDER SISTER   yeh. It is.

Beat.

YOUNGER SISTER …Sorry.

OLDER SISTER   Not enough.
                     Not good enough.
                     Not accepted Mary.
                     Not now. Not ever.

                     OLDER SISTER *sparks up her cigarette
                     alone and smokes.*

                     Pause.

YOUNGER SISTER …How many people signed my
                     petition…?

Nine

'The Child Soldier.'

The CHILD SOLDIER *sits next to his (the)* MUM *and* DAD,
passive.

MUM

MUM

MUM

DAD

MUM   His voice.

                     His voice –

DAD   What?

MUM   His voice –

DAD   there's nuthin nice about his / voice.

MUM   his voice –

DAD   there's nuthin nice about his voice – if
                     we're bein honest –

MUM	his tone and his… his softness and his… and how he'd call me and / use his…
DAD	There is nuthin nice about it – there is nuthin nice left about it.
MUM	His / voice –
DAD	His shoutin or his screamin voice?
MUM	His –
DAD	if we're bein honest – his screamin or his threatening voice?
MUM	As you're pinning him down or have you let him up by now?
DAD	His lyin voice or his cryin / voice?
MUM	How he speaks to me is different to how he speaks to you.
DAD	He doesn't speak.
MUM	To you.
DAD	He doesn't / speak
MUM	To you
DAD	he / doesn't.
MUM	how you speak to me –
DAD	he doesn't / speak
MUM	is disgraceful – he doesn't speak to me how you speak to me – how you speak to me is different to how I speak to you and how he speaks to me is different from that – we talk –
DAD	you don't talk.
MUM	We can talk.
DAD	Butchu don't.
MUM	I speak what I gotta / say –

DAD	I speak what I gotta say
MUM	you spit what you gotta say / back –
DAD	he doesn't speak he barks
MUM	to you.
DAD	He barks his demands and shouts his curses –
MUM	to you. He speaks to me
DAD	he shouts at you
MUM	at you
DAD	at you first
MUM	at you for bein you
DAD	at you for bein you and stinkin a that cheap shit still and still bein here when he weren't and losin him in the first fuckin / place –
MUM	I never lost (him) – they took –
DAD	*I* never lost him – screams at you for / that
MUM	and cursin me now are ya? Cursin at me now are ya?
DAD	I –
MUM	effin and blindin at me now are yer?
DAD	I'm sayin –
MUM	me or him is it this time? Which?
DAD	I'm just sayin –
MUM	me or him is it this time – which – cos I can't tell and it weren't / my –
DAD	you can spit your venom back –
MUM	it weren't my fault they took –
DAD	all you want –

MUM	they *took* him –
DAD	all you want, cos I sleep at night.
MUM	…Sit there sayin your shit
DAD	I can sleep at night – if we're bein / honest –
MUM	all your shit – in your shit – grunting in the corner.
DAD	When did you last have the full eight hours a the beauty / sleep?
MUM	I don't need / no –
DAD	Yeh you do –
MUM	I don't need no sleep – sleep ent what I / want
DAD	y'need somethin –
MUM	sleep ent what I / need
DAD	y'need somethin –
MUM	I don't sleep
DAD	see.
MUM	I can't sleep
DAD	see.
MUM	…If we're bein honest… I can't sleep. If we are bein that – if we're being that – are we being that?

Beat.

I can't sleep with him in the house…
I can't sleep with him back in the house.

Beat.

He scares me.

Ten

'Stoning Mary.'

OLDER SISTER   …Somethin fizzy.
                     Somethin fizzy 'n' strong.
                     Somethin that'd (*Gasps*.) me.
                     Bottles of it.
                     Crates a it.

                     No glass necessary suck it straight from
                     source, bottle up head back – lash it
                     down. Lovely. Lace me down like that.
                     …Somethin to the side… with somethin
                     good cooked to the side. Something
                     home-cooked to the side to go with and if
                     I was you – if you was me and I was you
                     – which we obviously ain't – but if we
                     was – and I wouldn't be in here where
                     you are if we did was that, but if we was
                     – an' how good would that be for you
                     havin a taste a how it is to be me, how
                     fuckin good it is to be me –

                     not

                     if I was you – I'd be well glad I weren't
                     me – but would be askin you for
                     somethin home cooked to go with.

                     Taste a my walk thru – thru what I go
                     thru cos a you…

                     If I was you I'd look at me and think
                     'shit' – look at me and think 'fuckin hell'
                     – look at me and thank fuck I weren't me
                     goin thru what I go thru cos a *you* – have
                     the bottle to give thanks to the church a

'fuckall' an' all over the that's-how-it-is.
If I was.
And if you was me and I was you...

Wouldn't be wearin them friggin things in
fronta my face for a start – prefer to look
sweet and squint, I would – I would –

YOUNGER SISTER If I was / you –

OLDER SISTER   if I was *you* – somethin home-cooked to
go with – if I was you I'd make you do
that cos you could cook, you could cook,
you always could cook – give you that –
couldn't yer?
Call you you'd do me a dish a somethin
on the homemade hot an' spectacular –
on the hypothetical that we're talkin –
somethin fancy to go with the crate a
fizzy that'd be feelin its way to fuckin me
up – thass what I'd do.

Thass what I'd do.
Thass what I'd want.
That's what I'd ask for – if I / was you.

YOUNGER SISTER If you was me and I was you I wouldn't
cook it.

Beat.

OLDER SISTER   ...Yeh you would.

YOUNGER SISTER ...I wouldn't.

OLDER SISTER   You would –

YOUNGER SISTER I / wouldn't.

OLDER SISTER   you would you would you would –

YOUNGER SISTER I wouldn't.

OLDER SISTER   I'd make yer.

YOUNGER SISTER I –

OLDER SISTER   I'd make yer I'd make yer. Wouldn't I.
                 Wouldn't I?

OLDER SISTER

OLDER SISTER

YOUNGER SISTER

YOUNGER SISTER …What if I never got your when-you-
                 rangs to say what cookin up you
                 wanted…

                 Never picked up. Never answered. Swear
                 down I never got the message. Swear
                 down more the VO never come…
                 Said I was out when I weren't…
                 Said I was away when I weren't…
                 Said I never got it when / I did…

OLDER SISTER   You tryinta be funny?

YOUNGER SISTER If I was that – you bein me, me bein you
                 – I couldn't cook yer nuthin if I never
                 heard nuthin from yer for years you'd
                 haveta think a somethin else then, haveta
                 think a someone else then…
                 Hypothetically speakin.

OLDER SISTER   See I – 'me-as-you' woulda allocated my
                 once a week to someone who would take
                 it. To someone who would wannit, as I'm
                 sure you – 'you-as-me' – would have told
                 your – 'me you' – from time. And if I
                 was you, I woulda clocked it and dialled
                 somewhere else.
                 Cos – 'you me' – mighta got sick and
                 tired a takin reverse charged allocated
                 anything from 'me you' – that 'you me'
                 didn't want – didn't ask for, and could
                 well do without.
                 Hypothetically friggin / speakin.

YOUNGER SISTER   What if your – 'you me' – never had no one else to call?

OLDER SISTER   I'd ask my 'me you' self why. If I was still *you*.
Which I wouldn't be…
Which I couldn't be.
Could I. Could I? Could I?
Andju wouldn't be my allocated call anyway.

YOUNGER SISTER   I wouldn't pick up.

OLDER SISTER   I know.

YOUNGER SISTER   I wouldn't be in.

OLDER SISTER   I know.

YOUNGER SISTER   I wouldn't come.

OLDER SISTER   See you juss answered your own next question then so don't bother askin why I didn't.

And twelve.

YOUNGER SISTER

YOUNGER SISTER   Twelve?

OLDER SISTER   Twelve people signed.

YOUNGER SISTER

OLDER SISTER   Put their pen to your petition. Twelve.

YOUNGER SISTER   Twelve's after ten, right?

OLDER SISTER   After eleven

YOUNGER SISTER   which is after ten, right?

OLDER SISTER

YOUNGER SISTER   How many did I need?

OLDER SISTER   Six thousand.

YOUNGER SISTER

YOUNGER SISTER

                  Pause.

OLDER SISTER   S'after a lotta tens / Mary.

YOUNGER SISTER   I know.

YOUNGER SISTER

YOUNGER SISTER

OLDER SISTER   Somethin fuckin fizzy to slowly fuck me up is what I'd ask for as my lass requess – thass my requess, would be my last request… if I was you.

                  Which I'm not.

                  So what is it you said to them you want as yourn?

                  Beat.

YOUNGER SISTER   You. To come.

Eleven

'The Child Soldier.'

MUM, SON (CHILD SOLDIER) *and* DAD.

Pause. Silence.

The SON *sniffs.*

DAD *smirks.*

The SON *sniffs again.*

SON *raises the game and sniffs more obviously.*

MUM *shifts. Uncomfortable.*

DAD *watches her, amused*.

DAD	You alright?… Love.
MUM	

SON *sniffs*.

DAD *enjoys* MUM*'s discomfort*.

MUM	
DAD	Are you?

SON *laughs a little*.

MUM	I'm…
	Is he…?
DAD	Why, I don't know. Is he?
MUM	…Is he alright?
DAD	…Are you alright?
SON	
DAD	He's 'fine'.
MUM	Is he?
DAD	Are yer?
MUM	He's not.
DAD	Are yer?
SON	Tell her to ask me.
MUM	
DAD	Ask him.
MUM	
SON	
DAD	
DAD	Ask him.

SON	Tell her to ask me
DAD	he says for you to…
MUM	
DAD	She says she –
SON	tell her to ask me.
DAD	He says for / you to –
MUM	Tell him I can't.
SON	Tell her she will.
	Beat.
DAD	…Why don't you ask him aye…?
	Just ask him how he is.
	SON *sniffs.*
	Ask him. Ask. Go on.
MUM	
MUM	
SON	
	Beat.
MUM	…How… are…
	How are…
	…*What-did-you-do…?*
	Pause.
SON	Tell her I am.
DAD	He says he –
SON	tell her I'm *fine.*
MUM	
SON	
SON	…Tell her she smells nice.

DAD	
DAD	
DAD	…He said… he said / you…
SON	Tell her.
DAD	…He said –
SON	*say it*.
MUM	Do I?

SON *smirks*.

Oh.

Twelve

'Stoning Mary.'

OLDER SISTER	What'll happen to them – what'll happen to them then?
YOUNGER SISTER	No one I know is gonna be there.
OLDER SISTER	What'll happen to them then? You gonna / wear them?
YOUNGER SISTER	You gonna / come?
OLDER SISTER	You gonna go out with them on – gonna go out there with them on you gonna go out lookin / like that?
YOUNGER SISTER	You comin?
OLDER SISTER	Picture in the paper – picture in the paper of you, of you out there – out there with / them on –
YOUNGER SISTER	They'll shave my head.

OLDER SISTER   I'd taken 'em off

YOUNGER SISTER   then strip me down

OLDER SISTER   I'd take 'em right off toldja

YOUNGER SISTER   then lead me out

OLDER SISTER   take 'em off – give 'em to charity

YOUNGER SISTER   are you gonna come?

OLDER SISTER   Give 'em to charity –

YOUNGER SISTER   cos they're expectin crowds

OLDER SISTER   – like some charity would want 'em.

YOUNGER SISTER   They're expectin crowds.
They're expectin a good crowd.
If they get good weather.
Get good weather they get good numbers.
So if you're comin. You gonna needta
book – if you're comin. Cos they gonna
charge.
But I can getchu a comp...
Cos you family.
They're expectin... (a good crowd)... if
it don't rain.
They're expectin... women's groups
block-booking almost booked it out – the
same bitches that wouldn't back me, the
same womens that wouldn't sign – them
same womens is block-bookin it out.
How many people marched for me?

OLDER SISTER

YOUNGER SISTER   More'n who signed for me?

OLDER SISTER

YOUNGER SISTER   ...Anybody march for me? How many
did that?

Less than ten?

OLDER SISTER   You spectin some stay of exe-somethin?

YOUNGER SISTER   Got no stay of exe-fuckin-nuthin have I.

                 …Not even the women. Not even the
                 women?

OLDER SISTER   …No.

YOUNGER SISTER   So what happened to the womanist
                 bitches?
                 …The feminist bitches?
                 …The professional bitches.
                 What happened to them?

                 What about the burn-their-bra bitches?
                 The black bitches
                 the rootsical bitches
                 the white the brown bitches
                 the right-on bitches
                 what about *them*?

                 What happened to the mainstream
                 bitches?
                 The rebel bitches
                 the underground bitches
                 what about – how 'bout –
                 the bitches that support other bitches?

                 Bitches that ain't but got nuthin better to do
                 bitches that gotta conscience
                 underclass bitches
                 overclass bitches
                 political bitches – what about – how
                 'bout –
                 what happened to *them*?

                 The bitches that love to march?
                 The bitches that love to study
                 the music-lovin bitches
                 the shebeen queen bitches
                 the bitches that love to fight
                 the bitches that love a debate

the bitches that love to curse?
The lyrical bitches
the educated bitches
the full-uppa-attitude bitches
the high-upsed rich-list lady bitch –
bitches
whadafuckabout them?

The bitches that love their men
the bitches that love other bitches' men
the bitches that juss love bitches –
what about alla them then?

…Not one a them would march for me?

OLDER SISTER

YOUNGER SISTER   Not a one a them would sign for me?

OLDER SISTER   …Well… twelve did.

YOUNGER SISTER   Where's all the bitches that'll support a
bitch, huh?
Out there supportin other bitches –
bitches that ain't me.
Where's all the bitches that'll protest a
bitch, eh?
Protestin for other bitches – bitches that
ain't me.
Bitches that can read.
Bitches that can count.
Pretty bitches.
Easy-on-the-eye bitches I betcha –

OLDER SISTER   butchu –

YOUNGER SISTER   but I'ma bitch in need

OLDER SISTER   butchu killed / a –

YOUNGER SISTER   I got cause

OLDER SISTER   you killed a man.

YOUNGER SISTER

YOUNGER SISTER And I'm gonna be stoned down for it.

OLDER SISTER

YOUNGER SISTER

OLDER SISTER You killed a man who was a boy.

YOUNGER SISTER …That *boy* was a soldier.

                Beat.

OLDER SISTER That soldier was a child –

YOUNGER SISTER that *child* killed my parents.
                Our parents, *ourn*.
                …I done somethin.
                Least I done somethin. I done somethin –
                I did. I did. I did – I done somethin.

YOUNGER SISTER

OLDER SISTER

YOUNGER SISTER Mum and Dad'd be – they would.

                Would've.

                They'da been prouda / me.

OLDER SISTER If they was here.

YOUNGER SISTER And they woulda been if he hadn't done
                what he did – ourn weren't his first, he'd
                killed other people – ourn weren't his
                first was they?

                Was they? Sis?

OLDER SISTER If they was here. They wouldn't come.
                Mum and Dad wouldn'ta come.

YOUNGER SISTER I wouldn't be in here for them to come to.

OLDER SISTER You wouldn't be in here for them to not
                come to.
                They wouldn'ta come.
                They couldn'ta come.

YOUNGER SISTER They would.

OLDER SISTER   They couldn't.

YOUNGER SISTER They would.

OLDER SISTER   They couldn't.

YOUNGER SISTER They would –

OLDER SISTER   they couldn't – not by now.

YOUNGER SISTER What?

                                        What?

OLDER SISTER

YOUNGER SISTER

YOUNGER SISTER What?

OLDER SISTER   Nuthin –

YOUNGER SISTER what?

OLDER SISTER

YOUNGER SISTER 'Nuthin'?

OLDER SISTER   Nuthin… No… Sis. 'Nuthin.'

OLDER SISTER

YOUNGER SISTER

                                        Beat.

                                        Betcha bitches'll come to my stonin, betchu they do.

                                        Betcha bitches'll come out for that tho.
Bring a bitch fuckin picnic and make the effort.
Dressed like a bitch on occasion as they watch.
Bet iss a bitch be first in the queue…

                                        Be first to fuckin throw…

Fuck it.
Fuck 'em.
Fuck them.
You gonna come – are you gonna come?

OLDER SISTER   I –

YOUNGER SISTER   you comin then? Comin then? You comin then – are yer?

OLDER SISTER

YOUNGER SISTER   You gonna come then? Are yer – are yer are yer ?

OLDER SISTER

YOUNGER SISTER   You are – you'll come you'll come you'll come won'tcha – won't yer – wont yer? You will – you will you will. Promise me. Promise me you'll come.

OLDER SISTER   …Are you gonna wear them?

YOUNGER SISTER

OLDER SISTER

OLDER SISTER *nods*.

YOUNGER SISTER

OLDER SISTER

YOUNGER SISTER   …Fuckin… twelve.

Thirteen

'The Child Soldier.'

MUM *is trying to cry.*

DAD

DAD

DAD

DAD   Ain't workin is it.

                       Ain't fallin is it. Are they?
                       Are they? Are they?

                       She did you your fuckin favour…

                       I know how dry your eyes were when he
                       was with us – and I can see how dry your
                       eyes are. Even now.

Fourteen

'The Prescription.'

O. SISTER EGO
BOYFRIEND EGO

OLDER SISTER
BOYFRIEND

BOYFRIEND   'We fightin?'

OLDER SISTER   'No.'

BOYFRIEND   'I ain't fightin.'

O. SISTER EGO	I said
OLDER SISTER	'You fightin me?'
BOYFRIEND EGO	Tell her –
BOYFRIEND	'No.'
O. SISTER EGO	(I) said
OLDER SISTER	'You're fightin me for it.'
BOYFRIEND	'I ain't fightin.'
O. SISTER EGO	Go on.
BOYFRIEND EGO	Go on.
O. SISTER EGO	He is.
BOYFRIEND EGO	She is.
OLDER SISTER	'You're fightin me for it. You are you are. You are tho – an' stand still – '
BOYFRIEND	'(You) come a bit closer (you) know that I can't – '
O. SISTER EGO	don't
OLDER SISTER	'can if you wanted to – '
BOYFRIEND EGO	again
BOYFRIEND	'(you) come a bit closer (you) know that I can't stand / still – '
O. SISTER EGO	no
OLDER SISTER	'nuthin but – '
O. SISTER EGO	nerves
BOYFRIEND	'what? 'Nuthin but' what? You put your hands on me you'd know.'
BOYFRIEND EGO	Carry on
BOYFRIEND	'put your hands on me to know'

OLDER SISTER	'don't needta toucha to tell how you're feelin.'
BOYFRIEND	'Feel me and find out.'
O. SISTER EGO	No.
BOYFRIEND EGO	Good. Good. Nice. Nice.
OLDER SISTER	'You forgettin how much I know yer – '
O. SISTER EGO	good
OLDER SISTER	'you forgettin I got the gift a seein how you – knowin how you are, know how you are before you do, know you that well don't I.'
BOYFRIEND	'(I) know *you* that well, don't I? Girlfriend.'
OLDER SISTER	'Boyfriend.'
BOYFRIEND	
OLDER SISTER	
O. SISTER EGO	C'mon…
OLDER SISTER	
O. SISTER EGO	*Come on.*
OLDER SISTER	
O. SISTER EGO	He reminds me –
OLDER SISTER	'You remind me – '
BOYFRIEND	'what?'
O. SISTER EGO	He reminds me –
OLDER SISTER	'You remind me – '
BOYFRIEND	'what?'
OLDER SISTER	'You remind me of my dad.'
BOYFRIEND EGO	What?

O. SISTER EGO	Good.
BOYFRIEND	'What – dyin of it like he did?'
OLDER SISTER	'He didn't get that far.
	Beat.
	Did he.'
BOYFRIEND	'I'm not fightin / you – '
OLDER SISTER	'But Dad woulda offered.'
BOYFRIEND	'I'm offerin to care for you.'
O. SISTER EGO	Shit.
BOYFRIEND EGO	Nice. Nicely done.
OLDER SISTER	'Let me care for you.'
BOYFRIEND EGO	No.
BOYFRIEND	'I'd care for you good.'
O. SISTER EGO	Yeh right.
OLDER SISTER	'I'd care for you better.'
BOYFRIEND EGO	Yeh right.
BOYFRIEND	'You can't care as careful as I can.
	Can you?'
OLDER SISTER	
O. SISTER EGO	He'd care?
OLDER SISTER	'You'd care?'
BOYFRIEND	'I'd care.'
OLDER SISTER	'Do yer care?'
BOYFRIEND	'I care.'
OLDER SISTER	'How much?'
BOYFRIEND	'I care – '

OLDER SISTER	'more'n me?'
BOYFRIEND EGO	Yeh yeh
BOYFRIEND	'I care'
OLDER SISTER	'more'n me? It is more'n me'
BOYFRIEND EGO	yeh
OLDER SISTER	'you are better'n me then'
BOYFRIEND EGO	I'm better'n you –
OLDER SISTER	'if you can care that much'
BOYFRIEND EGO	I am better
OLDER SISTER	'you be well better / than – '
BOYFRIEND	'it's not about – '
BOYFRIEND EGO	it is – and I am.
OLDER SISTER	'If you're gonna be there and be that care – full.'
BOYFRIEND	'Well – '
BOYFRIEND EGO	I am / better.
O. SISTER EGO	See
BOYFRIEND	'I do care – '
OLDER SISTER	'do yer?'
BOYFRIEND	'I do – '
OLDER SISTER	'how much?'
BOYFRIEND EGO	Much.
BOYFRIEND	'Much.'
OLDER SISTER	'How much?'
BOYFRIEND EGO	Much.
O. SISTER EGO	More'n I know?
BOYFRIEND	'More'n you know.'

OLDER SISTER EGO *smiles*.

OLDER SISTER | 'As much as – '

BOYFRIEND EGO | more'n that

OLDER SISTER | 'as much / as – '

BOYFRIEND | 'more'n you could know babes'

BOYFRIEND EGO | see

OLDER SISTER | 'as much as to let me have the prescription then?

As much as that…?

You can care as care – full as that?… As full a care as that for me?
Can you?

Then let me have the prescription.

…Please.'

BOYFRIEND

BOYFRIEND

OLDER SISTER EGO *smiles, triumphant*.

OLDER SISTER | 'Meds for me.
Me caring for you.
I would.
I would.
I could. I could. I could.

Long pause.

My dad wouldn'ta (fought).
My dad wouldn'ta fought for it.
Dad wouldn'ta fought my mum for it.
Wouldn'ta made her, fight for it.'

BOYFRIEND

OLDER SISTER

BOYFRIEND

OLDER SISTER

> BOYFRIEND *carefully picks up the prescription, then throws it on the ground in front of* OLDER SISTER.

O. SISTER EGO

OLDER SISTER

> *Beat.*

OLDER SISTER

OLDER SISTER

BOYFRIEND EGO   She's right.

BOYFRIEND

BOYFRIEND EGO   She is better at it than me.

Fifteen

'*Stoning Mary.*'

OLDER SISTER

OLDER SISTER

CORR. OFFICER

OLDER SISTER

CORR. OFFICER   …You said you would…

OLDER SISTER

CORR. OFFICER   You know she asked you to.

> I know she asked you to.

OLDER SISTER

OLDER SISTER

CORR. OFFICER   It's your sister. Bein stoned.

OLDER SISTER

CORR. OFFICER   And you promised / her.

OLDER SISTER   Have my ticket.

OLDER SISTER

OLDER SISTER   Take my ticket.

                 …I… don't wannit.

Sixteen

'Stoning Mary.'

(*The* CHILD SOLDIER*'s*) MUM *watches* MARY *for a while*.

MARY*'s head starts to be shaved down by the* CORRECTIONS OFFICER.

It rains.

MUM *picks up her first stone*.

End.

trade

August Wilson
(1945-2005)

Thank you
Peace

This version of *trade* was first performed by the Royal Shakespeare Company as part of the 2005 New Work Festival in the Swan Theatre, Stratford-upon-Avon, on 25 October 2005. The cast was as follows:

THE LOCAL	Lorna Brown
THE NOVICE	Nadine Marshall
THE REGULAR	Tanya Moodie
Director	Sacha Wares
Designer	Miriam Buether
Sound Designer	Paul Arditti

An earlier version of *trade* was performed by the Royal Shakespeare Company as part of the 2004 New Work Festival at The Other Place, Stratford-upon-Avon, in October 2004, and Soho Theatre, London, in March 2005. The cast was as follows:

THE LOCAL	Noma Dumezweni
THE NOVICE	Karen Bryson
THE REGULAR	Claire Benedict
Director	Sacha Wares

Characters

Three LOCAL *women*

Also:
The REGULAR *woman*
The NOVICE *woman*
BUMSTER
HOTELIER 1
HOTELIER 2
BREDRIN (*Guesthouse Staff and friend of Bumster*)
LOCAL MAN
AMERICAN TOURIST

All characters are played by three Black actresses.

Names appearing without dialogue indicate active silences between those characters.

/ punctuates the rhythm of a sentence.

(*Bracketed words*) *are the intention, not to be spoken by the character.*

LOCAL 1 *or* LOCAL 2 *indicate* 'LOCAL *woman' characters, but are played by the same actress who would play* NOVICE *or* REGULAR *respectively.*

LOCAL	Me.
LOCAL 1	Meh.
LOCAL 2	Me.
LOCAL 1	Her.
LOCAL 2	Her.
LOCAL	Me – mi juss –
LOCAL 2	mi juss –
LOCAL 1	we're juss –
LOCAL 2	'there'.
LOCAL	Local. All a we.
LOCAL 1	All a we three. *Local*.
LOCAL 2	Local to where them –
LOCAL	tek their holiday.
LOCAL 2	To where them –
LOCAL 1	haf their 'fun'.
LOCAL 2	To where them –
LOCAL 1	tek a break –
LOCAL	from who they are. From who they is. We 'local' to that. 'There.'
LOCAL 1	Me.
LOCAL 2	Meh.
LOCAL	Mi juss –
LOCAL 2	mi juss –
LOCAL 1	*we* juss live – 'there'. Local like that. 'There.' 'There' like that.

LOCAL	But them – 'the Novice.'
NOVICE	…What? So what?
LOCAL	Them – 'the Regular.'
REGULAR	What? So what?
LOCAL	Them touriss them: Regular, Novice. They bein that.
NOVICE	'The Regular.'
LOCAL	Old –
NOVICE	She looks
REGULAR	I'm not
LOCAL	she is
REGULAR	I'm not that –
NOVICE	old.
REGULAR	I'm not that –
LOCAL	'old' to me –
	also known as –
REGULAR	depends what
LOCAL	she is
REGULAR	what / what's meant by –
LOCAL	you are
REGULAR	meant by 'old'.
	'*Older*', yes –
LOCAL	The old / 'older' / white woman.
	'*The Regular Tourist.*'
	She bein that.
NOVICE	See.
	Beat.
REGULAR	I think –
LOCAL	see.
REGULAR	I / I / I think to myself… yeah / no / I / I / people that are –

LOCAL	like you
REGULAR	are / are –
NOVICE	like you
REGULAR	are / are / of / of / relationships that haven't worked / marriages maybe – maybe… maybe…
LOCAL	like you.
REGULAR	They're not / not gonna be young… very young / people.

NOVICE *and* LOCAL

        …No.

REGULAR	Are they?
LOCAL	
NOVICE	
REGULAR	Yeh. No / yes… Older –
LOCAL	old.
REGULAR	Yes. I… 'older'. I am.

        NOVICE *sniggers*.

        But at least I'm not… *her* (*Re:* NOVICE.)

LOCAL	The Novice.
NOVICE	What?
REGULAR	You.
NOVICE	*What?*
REGULAR	Least I'm not / no / not (that) –
LOCAL	'that'
REGULAR	that's right.
LOCAL	'*The Younger White Woman*.'

        The first-time-over-'there' – tourist. '*The Novice*.'

        She bein that.

        Her.

REGULAR	See. See with her, it's –
LOCAL	it's the –
NOVICE	iss a holiday / what?
LOCAL	The –
NOVICE	iss my holiday. What.
LOCAL	The –
NOVICE	I paid for it.
LOCAL	The –
NOVICE	*only I* paid for it.
LOCAL	The –
NOVICE	so I can do what I want.
	Beat.
	Beat.
	What? And why would I do – what? Why – what? *What* about me? So what about me – so fuckin what?
	Fuck you / fuck off.
REGULAR	Young.
NOVICE	Remember do ya?
REGULAR	See / young
NOVICE	remember that far back do yer? 'Regular.' Does she / bet she –
REGULAR	see.
LOCAL	Do yer?
NOVICE	Bet she don't.
LOCAL	
REGULAR	
NOVICE	And why would I do what I would do at home?
REGULAR	What do you do at home?

NOVICE	I'm not at home –
LOCAL	no y'not
NOVICE	why would I wanna do that? Why would I do what I do back 'here' when I ain't 'here' – don't make no sense – I'm not at *home* / am I / am I?
REGULAR	(*Unimpressed.*) No.
LOCAL	You're 'there' –
REGULAR	on holiday
NOVICE	I am
LOCAL	she is
REGULAR	yes. She is.
	LOCAL *kisses her teeth.*
NOVICE	I'm not 'here' / I'm 'there'. Yeh? Why would I do what I always do? Why would I – would I *not* do what I wouldn't do at home? I'm 'there' / I am / I'm 'there' –
LOCAL	nah mek no fockin sense –
REGULAR	great. I go 'there' / on holiday 'there' / to get away –
NOVICE	from 'here'
REGULAR	to get away from –
NOVICE	'here'
REGULAR	to get away from –
LOCAL	people like –
REGULAR	her. People like –
NOVICE	who?
LOCAL	People like –
REGULAR	that.
LOCAL	People like –
NOVICE	what?

REGULAR   People like –

LOCAL *and* REGULAR
                 you.

REGULAR   People like *you* / that are 'here'.

                 I go 'there' to get away from that.

NOVICE   Least I ain't / I ain't / see…

REGULAR   What?

                 What?

NOVICE   '*That.*' (*Re:* REGULAR.)

REGULAR   What?

NOVICE   *Her.*

REGULAR   What?

LOCAL   Yet.

NOVICE   Nah – never / I just –

LOCAL   yu 'juss' is juss enough –

REGULAR   exactly.

NOVICE   What?

                 REGULAR *is amused.*

LOCAL   See. *I* just –

REGULAR   I know

LOCAL   I juss – mi juss

REGULAR *and* NOVICE
                 we know

NOVICE   I saw yer

REGULAR   I saw you –

LOCAL   mi juss… mi juss / live here.

NOVICE   The Local.

REGULAR   '*The Local.*'

NOVICE   She busy been bein that.

LOCAL   I saw you. Si yu. Them.

NOVICE	'Local Styles at Local Prices.'
	Like your sign. (*Dry*.) I saw that.
LOCAL	'Hair on the beach. Getchur hair done on the beach – getchur hair did done good' – thass mi
NOVICE	plaits for payment – thass you
LOCAL	'the quickest, si mi, Miss Quick Finger – si mi? Canerow fe cash' – thass me
REGULAR	'I don't know…'
LOCAL	'a change a style'
REGULAR	'I don't know… '
LOCAL	(*Dry*.) 'try something new'
REGULAR	'I just don't – '
LOCAL	(*Dry*.) 'live a likkle… iss juss hair.'
REGULAR	'I don't / I mean – '
LOCAL	(*Not convinced*.) 'it could suit – '
NOVICE	nah it couldn't.
REGULAR	(*Not convinced*.) 'You think – ?'
NOVICE	nah it couldn't
REGULAR	(*Not convinced*.) ' – well… '
NOVICE	No
LOCAL	(*Lying*.) 'Y'noh – '
NOVICE	nah
REGULAR	'maybe and like / like / like how – '
LOCAL	like –
REGULAR	'like how Bo Derek – '
NOVICE	like how Becks –
LOCAL	(*Weary*.) like how *we* do.
NOVICE	'Quick Finger.' You do what you do.
LOCAL	Mi do what mi do.

NOVICE	You do that.
LOCAL	Mi do what mi do –
	mi do what mi do well.
	Mi noh mi do hair well.
	Even your something that straight something.
	Straight up.
	A straight-up-and-down… h'economic transaction.
	Like that.
LOCAL	
NOVICE	Like a drink.
REGULAR	Like that.
LOCAL	
REGULAR	Like a meal.
NOVICE	Like that.
REGULAR	Like –
NOVICE	like / see / uh / like like a drink – a drink in a bar.
REGULAR	Like the *offer* of a drink in a bar –
NOVICE	like a meal –
	LOCAL *kisses her teeth.*
REGULAR	like the *offer* of a meal –
NOVICE	like the –
	(*As* BUMSTER.) '*I… y'know – mi see yu – *'
	Like the –
REGULAR	(*As* BUMSTER.) '*Mi see yu… y'noh… saw you from before – .*'
	Like the –

NOVICE	(*As* BUMSTER.) '*I… see yu / saw you from before… and… and tho't unoo was…*'
LOCAL	What?
REGULAR	(*As* BUMSTER.) '*tho't you was –* '
NOVICE	What?
LOCAL	Tho't them was *what*?
REGULAR	He thought I was… (*As* BUMSTER.) '*…nice…*'
LOCAL	
NOVICE	
NOVICE	(*As* BUMSTER.) '*Barman! Mek mi order the lady a…* '
REGULAR	(*As* BUMSTER.) '*Waiter! Mek mi order the lady a…* '
NOVICE	(*To* LOCAL.) A straight-up-and-down economic –
LOCAL	emotional
NOVICE	economic transaction. Yeh?
	Like that.
	Yeah?
	And 'Nice'?
	Beat.
REGULAR	I / I / it's not that… I haven't / y'know –
NOVICE	no
REGULAR	y'know
LOCAL	no
NOVICE	what?
LOCAL	Know what?
REGULAR	I / uh –
NOVICE	(*As* BUMSTER.) '*nice –* '

REGULAR	been called – for… (ages)… haven't been called for… ages
LOCAL	so him call yu –
NOVICE	(*As* BUMSTER.) '*nice* – '
LOCAL	yu let him call yu –
NOVICE	nice
LOCAL	it sweet yu to be called –
REGULAR	'Nice' / I / uh / haven't been called for… years.

Beat.

I haven't been called anything for years.

I haven't called myself / even / well you (don't) / for / uh / for / for… for… years.

NOVICE	'Nice'?

'Nice' came with the drink?

'Nice' came with the drink did it?'

LOCAL	'Nice'… ice and a slice –
NOVICE	'Nice' was what did it was it?
LOCAL	Transacted / executed / and accepted –

the drink. And the compliment.

Easy.

NOVICE	Nice and easy.
LOCAL	She is.

Emotional.

Emotionally easy.

You are.

REGULAR	I –
LOCAL	Juss too easy –

(*Re:* NOVICE.) you are.

NOVICE *ups middle finger to* LOCAL *and* REGULAR.

	Nu'un nice about that. Is there.
NOVICE	(*Re:* REGULAR.) For years…?
	Beat.
	You ent – 'nice' – not for no years?
REGULAR	
NOVICE	
NOVICE	Really…?
	Really?
	Shit.
	NOVICE *is amused.*
REGULAR	I haven't / I haven't got (anyone)…
NOVICE	(*To* LOCAL.) Ere what – she ain't got –
REGULAR	got… anyone –
NOVICE	(*To* LOCAL.) ere what –
REGULAR	who is there to say it?…
NOVICE	(*To* LOCAL.) She ain't – not for no *years*!
REGULAR	I have no one to say it… So / so why would I feel it?
NOVICE	Say it 'bout myself all the time / say it to myself all the time –
LOCAL	I'd tell yu 'bout –
NOVICE	geddit said 'bout myself all the time –
LOCAL	I'd tell yu 'boutchu self –
NOVICE	gettem to tell me 'bout myself / all the time –
LOCAL	I'd tell you boutcha self –
NOVICE	you wouldn't be who I'd be askin.
LOCAL	Yu askin the wrong people then –
NOVICE	don't think so darlin / but you… (*Re:* REGULAR.) y'know / if you want summat

to feel / feel yourself – feel it yourself /
you want someone to say it / waitin on
someone to say it / say it yourself / say it to
y'self – what?

Y'know / cos y'know / you / uh / I / you /
you look… suppose / you / y'know…
maybe – y'know / you could –

LOCAL   what part?

NOVICE   You do look… sorta…

LOCAL   She don't.

NOVICE   She could look sorta –

LOCAL   she don't tho

NOVICE   could – nice.

REGULAR   Do I?

LOCAL   No.

NOVICE   Yeh… in… a sorta –

REGULAR   do I?

LOCAL   She don't

NOVICE   sorta 'old' – sorta way.

REGULAR

NOVICE

REGULAR   …Should I thank you?

NOVICE   You tell me.

REGULAR   When I need some self / self-help –

NOVICE   just sayin –

REGULAR   when I need some life lessons / uh /
               lessons in life –

NOVICE   tryinta be helpful –

REGULAR   when I need some advice –

NOVICE   I geddit –

REGULAR   I won't come to you.

NOVICE	
REGULAR	
NOVICE	I just paid you a compliment.
	Or don't my compliment count (then) – ?
LOCAL	As much as his musta.
	Beat.
	The drink.
REGULAR	A drink.
NOVICE	(*As* BUMSTER.) '*Barman! Ah said – lemme order the lady a…*'
LOCAL	highballed glass a flattery.
REGULAR	He bought me a –
NOVICE	(*As* BUMSTER.) '*Barman! I said mek mi order the lady a –* '
LOCAL	highballed glass a attention.
REGULAR	So what.
LOCAL	Laced with sweet talk?
REGULAR	Sweetness.
LOCAL	Lyrics?
REGULAR	Loveliness –
LOCAL	loveliness? Bullshit.
	And she *still* looks –
REGULAR	I looked how he made me feel –
LOCAL	*still* looks old to me.
REGULAR	How I felt for once –
NOVICE	once?
	Look like she loved it / ere what / don't she – looks like you'd love it / looks like you love it / loved it.
	Y'look like you landed / landed somethin / and lovin it – ere what – focus on a

female's face long enough – can feel how long since she been – 'felt' / how long since you been 'felt'? / How long since you felt / felt since you been – been since you been (fucked) – since she been (fucked) –

REGULAR   excuse (me) – *what*

NOVICE   focus on this one's face long enough –

REGULAR   excuse – no –

LOCAL   (*As* BUMSTER.) '*Yu noh si how yu look "nice" –* '

REGULAR   look – don't –

NOVICE   give it that – and look how this one looks –

REGULAR   look I don't –

NOVICE   you do

REGULAR   don't need you to –

NOVICE   you do / ere what / she does / this one – y'know what – you do / you look… this one looks –

REGULAR   I / I / you know / uh –

NOVICE   – *fresh!* Fresh.

REGULAR   Is this more of your / is this more of *her* philosophy?

NOVICE   Focus on her for a minute –

REGULAR   she can / *you* can keep it –

NOVICE   focus on you for a minute / can see that / can see something / can see someone's been freshly… fucked.

NOVICE *is amused.*

REGULAR   …The sea –

LOCAL   'bout 'the sea'.

REGULAR   The sea –

NOVICE   thass right / the not bein 'here' –

REGULAR	the sand –
LOCAL	'bout 'the sand'.
NOVICE	Thass right / the bein over 'there' –
REGULAR	the sun –
LOCAL	'bout 'the sun'
NOVICE	thass right / the I gotta tan to work on.
REGULAR	The –
NOVICE	the that –
REGULAR	the –
NOVICE	the what?
REGULAR	The –
LOCAL	the age gap.
LOCAL	
REGULAR	
REGULAR	Before I could / y'know / tell myself –
NOVICE	what? 'Nice'?
REGULAR	Before I would –
LOCAL	'tell yourself' – what?
REGULAR	It does / I just / uh / y'know… he could tell – he could tell –
LOCAL	what hotel you was stayin in
REGULAR	he *did* tell me –
LOCAL	high end, low end
REGULAR	tell me / before I would tell myself –
LOCAL	before your highball glass a bullshit was drained dry he could tell that – if he'd done him job right / was doin his –
NOVICE	job?
LOCAL	Job right.
NOVICE	(*To* REGULAR.) Bitter.

LOCAL	Bitter?
NOVICE	Bitter. Leave her. Go on.
REGULAR	…Before I would tell myself – 'nice' / nice. He… uh / did. And I would / I wouldn't tell myself / that / and that's the / prob / part of the problem / but – and – he could tell
LOCAL	what flight unoo drop out the sky from
REGULAR	and did before anyone would tell me / he told me
LOCAL	package or charter
REGULAR	he told me in two days 'there' what nobody 'here' has said in – years…
	He could –
LOCAL	tell if yu was a credit-card or cash kinda / high-end / low-end kinda / t'ree-week or two kinda / single or not kinda… h'investment.
NOVICE	He could (tell) –
LOCAL	tell if you was German or Canadian or Canadian or English or… English or American –
NOVICE	he could tell you was a (good un) –
REGULAR	do I look American? / I don't look American…
NOVICE	You don't look American
LOCAL	– is what he musta thought.
	Americans give too much –
	(*As* BUMSTER.) '*The American dem – dem gi it too much – too much of the… mout / too much a the h'attitude –* '
	he said.
	'*Ent really givin when it comes to givin is it*' is they?

	He said.
	'*Too much like hard work.*'
	Ent they?
	And why struggle wid that when what he's got before him is more likely to give… give it up.
REGULAR	Not nice.
LOCAL	(*As* BUMSTER.) '*Fe free.*'
NOVICE	Not nice
LOCAL	y'not
REGULAR	not true
LOCAL	for the price of a highball glass of su'un sweet then, right?
	Ice – slice an' a 'nice' –
REGULAR	it's not like that.
LOCAL	No?
REGULAR	No.
NOVICE	Maybe she's not like that. She said –
LOCAL	before you even finished your first straight-up-and-down-highballed-economic-transaction-of-a-drink / he had you sussed. Sussed – clocked an' categorise. *Thass* what that was for. Thass what you were for.
	And yes – 'job' – and *yes* – him could tell –
NOVICE	thass what / ere what – *thass what* / right / what holidays is for. What getting away is for – getting away from it is for – takin time out is for – vacations is – breaks is for – yeah?
	Begrudgin me / us – begrudgin us a little a – *I work* – we work –

LOCAL	s'mody employ *you*?
NOVICE	*We* work –
REGULAR	you know nothing about me –
NOVICE	work hard for this – and you / *you* / see / you –
REGULAR	yes, you
NOVICE	you're juss playin –
REGULAR	you are
NOVICE	playin bitter
REGULAR	you are
NOVICE	bitter and backward wiv it – ain't she? – Ain't she –
	REGULAR *nods*.
	and when did somebody last tell you / *you* / see / you that *you* / huh? / You looked '*nice*'?
REGULAR	Yeh.
NOVICE	Right.
REGULAR	Yes.
NOVICE	See
REGULAR	yes
NOVICE	see!
REGULAR	
NOVICE	
LOCAL	When *he* did.
	Before him tell you… that you did.
	Beat.
NOVICE	
REGULAR	
LOCAL	Who paid fi yu second drink?

	Who paid for the third?
REGULAR	
NOVICE	
	LOCAL *laughs to herself.*
LOCAL	Wha? Yu noh haf nu'un f'seh? Cyat ketch yu tongue?
	Or su'un else.
NOVICE	Fuck it / me? I juss took the drink and drank it / so what?
	…Do it over 'here' / so I'm not gonna not do it over 'there' am I?
REGULAR	You said.
NOVICE	Thass right – what? I'm on holiday 'there' –
REGULAR	you've said.
NOVICE	Thass right.
LOCAL	Yu said.
NOVICE	He offered –
LOCAL	who paid for your second drink?
REGULAR	(*To* LOCAL.) Anybody ever offer *you* anything?
LOCAL	Who paid f'the second drink?
NOVICE	He said / (*As* BUMSTER.) '*This is for you.*'
	I said / 'I never asked for no drink.'
	He said / (*As* BUMSTER.) '*Yu not gonna not drink it now / y'know?*'
	I said / 'I never asked for no drink tho.'
	(He) givin it / (*As* BUMSTER.) '*Now that I bought it / bought it fi yu –* '
	(I) said / 'But did I ask for a drink – '
	(*As* BUMSTER.) '*I know yu not gonna do me like that.*'

	'You're blockin my sun – '
REGULAR	yes, alright –
NOVICE	he said / (*As* BUMSTER.) '*You was blockin mi view – *'
REGULAR	I think we (get it) –
NOVICE	'I was tryinta top up my tan'
	(He) gives it / (*As* BUMSTER.) '*improvin on mi view / blockin an' improvin – *'
REGULAR	*alright –*
NOVICE	I said –
LOCAL	I'm sayin who paid for the *next* drink / who paid for your drink after that?
NOVICE	How'dya know there was one?
REGULAR	One?
NOVICE	…Some.
LOCAL	There would be.
	Wu'udnt there.
	If he was doin his 'job' – right.
	Cah, yu h'English like a drink. Don't it.
	Tek a drink. Don't it.
	Like the taste a drink…
	Don't it –
REGULAR	excuse me –
NOVICE	nah I'll deal wiv her – see I – / I'll deal wiv her – see *I* – ain't one a them / ain't one a them Faliraki-out-on-the-piss-out-for-days-out-of-me-head-all-night-type-a-traveller.
	I don't do *that*.
	Vomitin up the place / embarrassin yourself –
	I don't do that.

In a right state from touchdown to departure –

I don't do that.

Ere what – off your tits – happy to be hungover for me whole of me holiday? See / *I* don't do *that*…

…Any more.

REGULAR *raises her eyes to the skies.*

And *she* don't look the fuckin type –

REGULAR   er / excuse me but –

NOVICE   ere wot / y'know what – trust me. You don't.

LOCAL *laughs to herself.*

LOCAL   After your first glass a flattery / he ent got no intention a payin fe the rest. Bet you offered… bet him get you to offer – bet you tho't you was offerin off your own-ah back – bet him get you to do that – bet you *said* –

NOVICE   you don't know what I said –

REGULAR   you don't know me

LOCAL   betchu said –

REGULAR   you wouldn't know what I said / she wouldn't –

NOVICE   nah she won't / no one gets me to say nuthin I don't wanna –

LOCAL   yu sure

NOVICE   no one gets me to do nuthin I don't wanna –

REGULAR   nothing?

NOVICE   Nuthin.

REGULAR   Never?

NOVICE   Nah never.

REGULAR	Young. I told you.
LOCAL	Young. She is.
NOVICE	Nobody's gonna tell me nuthin / nobody can tell me nuthin / no man can tell me nuthin / them days is over.
	Where *we're* from. Yeh?
	Yeah?
REGULAR	What – ?
NOVICE	Where 'we' from (yeah) – so don't be sayin 'bout what I said / cos you wouldn't know / how would you know?
	You don't know / see – quiet – see?
	Be quiet. See?!
	Where we are from – dunno 'bout here – *darlin* – but where we been / where we come from / we been thru the women's thing / we don't get bossed it no more – where *we're* from, yeh?
	Yeah.
	We / past all that / we been thru – well – I never went thru it meself / that was more like her generation / her lot – / runnin up an' down the place marchin an shit / we been thru that / you burn your bra didja? Chain yourself to the fences and shit –
REGULAR	What / for / uh / your benefit?
NOVICE	See / bet she did / tits hangin low as she was battlin 'gainst the pigs / bra burnt to bits as she's chained to some fuckin…
REGULAR	suffragettes
NOVICE	I suffer too / we / our generation have our own sufferin –
REGULAR	which were a / uh / different battle to –
NOVICE	I know / history / I know – our history / an' I couldn't be lettin my shit go / my tits go /

	thass askin a bit too much of the bit too much / but / my point is –
REGULAR	oh God
NOVICE	where *we're* from –
REGULAR	we're not from the same place –
NOVICE	*country* – not manor / no –
REGULAR	we couldn't be from the same place –
LOCAL	glad we not from the same place –
NOVICE	where *we're* from… no man can't tell / can't tell me – we – *us* –
REGULAR	well
NOVICE	'bout our business / and what to-fuckin-do. Right.
LOCAL	Ev'ryting equal – where *you're* from –
NOVICE	thass right
LOCAL	man and woman equal-righted – where you're from
NOVICE	thass right
REGULAR	well –
LOCAL	equal-righted / human-righted – a he an' she same-way-righted / right?
NOVICE	Right.
LOCAL	Where you're from.
NOVICE	Yep.
REGULAR	Well –
LOCAL	so righted / so right / so righteously right-on yu ha fe find yu'self alfway round the fockin world to find back the kinda man you equal-righted right outta h'existence.
	…Right?
	Beat.

NOVICE	…Right / you deal with her –
REGULAR	what?
LOCAL	Right.
REGULAR	Equality –
NOVICE	right –
LOCAL	man is man an' ooman iss ooman 'cept yu noh satisfied wid that – noh satisfied wid what yu fought for –
REGULAR	equal rights –
NOVICE	right –
LOCAL	be careful whatchu h'ask for –
NOVICE	no – now what / see what – now / look – what / look what she's doin – she's lookin to confuse –
LOCAL	noh hard
NOVICE	lookin to confuse the –
LOCAL	noh hard
NOVICE	lookin to confuse *me* –
REGULAR	isn't hard.
LOCAL	Yu there lookin the kinda man you lookin to like / like to like / like likin our man's dem… right.
	Thass your… human right. Right?
	Where's mine.
NOVICE	
LOCAL	
NOVICE	…A fuckin drink / right.
REGULAR	Right.
NOVICE	And I offered cos I could
LOCAL	equality…
NOVICE	I paid / cos I could.

LOCAL	Real likkle feminiss
NOVICE	cos *I* wanted to.
	Cos I can.
	Cos –
LOCAL	'you're on holiday.'
	(*Amused.*) He is good / gotcha thinkin that.
NOVICE	Cos he bought me one first – cos I could... Cos I said '*I'll treat yer*' –
	LOCAL *is amused.*
	What?
	Beat.
LOCAL	(*To* REGULAR.) After *your* first glass a flattery... Bet *you* offered... betchu did –
REGULAR	*I* offered because I could.
	I paid / because I could.
	Because I wanted to.
	Because I can.
	Because – and / I'm not / I – I'm not going to –
NOVICE	nah don't.
REGULAR	I'm not going to justify –
NOVICE	nah don't –
REGULAR	I'm not – to you –
NOVICE	nah *don't* –
REGULAR	I'm not going to ridicule the
LOCAL	what?
REGULAR	...Romance –
NOVICE	what?
LOCAL	'Romance'?
REGULAR	...Romance of it.

NOVICE	Get your romance at home – fuck that
REGULAR	there is no romance at home
LOCAL	not our problem
NOVICE	fuck that.
REGULAR	The romance – I'm not like you –
NOVICE	I'm not like *you*
REGULAR	you couldn't be like me.
NOVICE	
REGULAR	When did you last –
LOCAL	walk by the water?
NOVICE	So no.
REGULAR	Stare at the stars –
NOVICE	so fuckin no
LOCAL	(*Dry.*) hand hold?
REGULAR	While he held you / yes
LOCAL	(*Mocking.*) and dance?
NOVICE	Dance? You / dance?
REGULAR	And… yes / I / uh… dance…
NOVICE	Fuck –
REGULAR	when did you last –
NOVICE	that. *Right*. Off. I came to –
REGULAR	do that?
NOVICE	I came to –
LOCAL	fuck?
NOVICE	
LOCAL	
NOVICE	I ain't a one to get fucked over, darlin. Trust me.
LOCAL	What? That how somebody did do you back home then?

	LOCAL *and* NOVICE *eyeball*.
NOVICE	And romance ain't my reality.
LOCAL	You said.
REGULAR	That's you.
	He bought me an unasked-for appreciated drink.
	We ate together – that's me.
LOCAL	Who did pay?
REGULAR	He bought me a – I asked –
LOCAL	who did paid (for) –
REGULAR	that's not the point.
LOCAL	That is the point.
	That was his point.
	Thass business.
	Thass his business / thass good business / ent that good business, lady?
	If thass all the business he got?
LOCAL	
REGULAR	
NOVICE	
LOCAL	What – yu noh able to be the women yu wanna be over your 'there' or what?
	That why you come over to our 'here' is it?
	To be what you think you could be / not admittin to what you are?
NOVICE	Iss a holiday / yeh?
LOCAL	Or you still workin on who you are 'there' / haveta come over to 'here' to flex it –
REGULAR	it's a / (holiday). That's (all) –
LOCAL	tekkin a break from who you are 'there' by comin over to my 'here' – what – you disappoint yourself 'there'?

NOVICE *ups middle finger to* LOCAL.

NOVICE   Not as much as your mother mus be
          disappointed with you.

LOCAL

NOVICE

LOCAL   You got a mudder?

NOVICE

LOCAL   She like you?

NOVICE   You ain't talkin 'bout my mum –

REGULAR   Ladies –

NOVICE   she talkin 'bout my mum?

LOCAL   Look like it don't it –

NOVICE   you bringin my mum into this?

LOCAL   Well – *look* like it don't it.

REGULAR   Ladies –

LOCAL   'ladies' where? Not what they call yu (*Re:*
          NOVICE.) – not what they call y'mudder –

NOVICE   you fuckin / like you'd fuckin / she wants
          to leave my fuckin mother –

REGULAR   I don't think you should talk about her
          (mother) –

LOCAL   (*To* REGULAR.) you tellin mi what mi can
          and mi cyant (say) –

NOVICE   she don't know / know nuthin 'bout my –

LOCAL   (*To* REGULAR.) *yu* – tryinta censorise
          meh?

NOVICE   Mention her again / make her mention / let
          her mention my fuckin mother again –

LOCAL   mention your fuckin 'what' again?

NOVICE   Fuckin do it – fuckin / go on / go on / *do it*

LOCAL   'fuckin mudder'… mother fucker…

NOVICE

LOCAL

> NOVICE *eyeballs* LOCAL.
>
> What? You is like her?
>
> You favour ar?
>
> She muss be like her… don't she.

NOVICE

LOCAL

NOVICE   I'm *not* like her.

> I'm not.

REGULAR

NOVICE

LOCAL

NOVICE   Why don't you take a break from your mouth… Yeh? Why don'tchu take a break from who you are Miss Canerow-for-Cash / why don'tchu take a break from your 'getchure hair done on the fuckin beach' bullshit – and. See. I come 'there' cos I can.

And I come 'there' cos I (can) – / ere what / I come 'there' cos it's beautiful / and I come 'there' cos I ain't been before / and I come 'there' cos I worked hard / saved up / and me and my girls wanted to. *Right*. I come there cos it looked propah picture-perfect in the catalogue / and I come 'there' cos it read that the 'locals' is… so… fuckin… *friendly*.

NOVICE

LOCAL

NOVICE   Iss a holiday / recommend you take one.

LOCAL   …I would / if I could –

NOVICE	I ent joinin your pity party so don't invite me.
REGULAR	Why would you want to go on holiday?
	You don't need to go on holiday…
	You don't need to go anywhere else…
	When where you are is so lovely…
LOCAL	
REGULAR	Er… / Uh…
NOVICE	I done scuba-dived 'there' / which I wouldn't do at home / I done windsurfin 'there' – which I wouldn't do at home / I been on a boat / which I wouldn't do at home / I ate things / I drank things / I seen things what I wouldn't do at home / and I –
LOCAL	fucked a local
REGULAR	which you wouldn't do at home.
NOVICE	(*To* REGULAR.) Pot. Kettle. Black. Yeah?
	And I ain't one a them sand slags / come over 'there' / what? / Come over 'there' / and fuck whatever / I ain't one a them 'different-one-every-nighters' / nah / yeh? I done what I didn't do at home –
LOCAL	what she wouldn't do at home
NOVICE	I knew what I was doin / an' I dunnit / so what –
LOCAL	or didju get done?
NOVICE	Toldja. People don't do me, I do them.
REGULAR	Philosophy. Mind / uh / mind you don't hurt yourself –
LOCAL	Do the drinks tho dontchu?
	That's the point / thass my point.
REGULAR	What?

NOVICE	Ere what / I don't care –
LOCAL	thass my point –
NOVICE	care boutcha 'points'. There is no point.
	You have no point.
	She has no – .
	Bitter.
LOCAL	What?
NOVICE	(*To* REGULAR.) See what I said? Bitter.
REGULAR	What?
LOCAL	Bitter.
REGULAR	I moved hotels.

LOCAL *and* NOVICE

What?

Beat.

REGULAR	Because I… (could.)
	Because I… / uh… could…
NOVICE	
LOCAL	
NOVICE	Y'moved hotels? She moved hotels?
	What for? / Summat wrong with it? Something wrong with her? It never had nuthin or summat / never had no air-con or nuthin –
LOCAL	You get –
NOVICE	what you movin for?
LOCAL	Y'get throwed out?
NOVICE	Didja?
LOCAL	Heh.
NOVICE	(*As* HOTELIER 1.) '*Y'know / this my business / our business / our fambily business –* '

LOCAL	yu get – ?!
NOVICE	(*As* HOTELIER 1.) ' – *most of the peoples that come to this place* / *my place* / *my place that is our place* / *this place that is our* – *h'establishment* / *y'know* / *our hotel* – '
LOCAL	(*Amused*.) yu did!
NOVICE	(*As* HOTELIER 1.) '*They is* / *they are* – *couples* / *um* / *they are married* / *er fambilies* / *y'know…?*'
LOCAL	(*Amused*.) Them dash yu.
REGULAR	Er –
NOVICE	(*As* HOTELIER 1.) '*Y'know* / *I* / *uh… can't have you here…* both *of you here.*'
REGULAR	
	LOCAL *laughs*.
NOVICE	(*As* HOTELIER 1.) '*If you're gonna be* / *uh… doin that.*'
	Go on.
LOCAL	Go on.
NOVICE	*Go on.*
REGULAR	…I moved hotels / what / I / I mean / what / but what –
LOCAL	(*As* HOTELIER 2.) '*Year roun* / *year roun* / *year roun* – *year round we get the* / *bookins that we get year round* – '
NOVICE	(*Amused*.) 'but what' – there ain't no 'but what' –
REGULAR	I just – we wanted to / I mean / but / what – type of hotel was I in –
LOCAL	(*As* HOTELIER 2.) '*Canadian an' British* / *German an' British* / *British an'* – *year roun year* – '

REGULAR	What type of hotel was I in?
LOCAL	(*As* HOTELIER 2.) '*Nuff a them…*
	…But. We still – nah – tek – yu.
	We can't take you. Here.
	Doin that.
	Here.
	Wid him.'
REGULAR	What type of hotel are you in – .
	What type of hotel are you in / that won't let / let their own in?
LOCAL	Dash out.
REGULAR	What kind of place is that?
NOVICE	Thrown out?
REGULAR	What kind of –
NOVICE	thass why I stayed put.
REGULAR	I moved hotels –
LOCAL	to one that would?
REGULAR	
LOCAL	To one that would.
REGULAR	
LOCAL	To one that would letchu…
NOVICE	Don't do them ones what let them locals in.
LOCAL	(*To* REGULAR.) On whose recommendation?
	Beat.
	LOCAL *smiles knowingly.*
NOVICE	I paid to be there / the air-con / the room service / that's where I'm stayin / I'm stayin put –
REGULAR	

LOCAL	
NOVICE	without them stayin over – what – what? / What – .
REGULAR	
LOCAL	
NOVICE	What? You two havin a moment?
LOCAL	(*To* REGULAR.) On whose recommendation?
	(*As* BUMSTER.) '*Bredrin. Tings cool?*'
NOVICE	(*As* BREDRIN, *guesthouse staff who knows* BUMSTER.) '*Tings cool. Busy.*'
LOCAL	(*As* BUMSTER.) '*Yu manager?*'
NOVICE	(*As* BREDRIN.) '*Him cool. Busy.*'
LOCAL	(*As* BUMSTER.) '*Still cool wid me?*'
NOVICE	(*As* BREDRIN.) '*Still cool wid yu. Dollars dem ah talk / bullshit still ah walk. Paid room is a paid room. We gotta guesthouse to fill… dollar?*'
LOCAL	(*As* BUMSTER.) '*Strickly US*'
	NOVICE *is amused.*
REGULAR	He / well / he obviously / y'know… knows… the place / places… better than I do.
LOCAL	Exactly.
REGULAR	We. I. Rented a guesthouse… it was –
NOVICE	what?
REGULAR	It was –
LOCAL	cheap?
REGULAR	It was –
NOVICE	cheaper?
REGULAR	It was lovely.

NOVICE	(*Dry*.) Great.
LOCAL	'Lovely.' From the 'nice' / to the / 'lovely'.
	(*Dry*.) Wicked.
	NOVICE *is amused*.
REGULAR	And how did / I / uh / I'm not being funny / but… how… how did you afford to / *could* you afford to… buy anybody a second and third anything? / Look at *you* –
NOVICE	enjoy the view –
REGULAR	look at her.
NOVICE	Hard currency baby –
LOCAL	look 'pon ar
NOVICE	hard currency (baby) –
REGULAR	you're playing at being what you're not –
NOVICE	and you are…?
REGULAR	You're playing at what you could never be at home.
NOVICE	And you are?
REGULAR	You're playin at what you could never afford to be –
NOVICE	I'm only bein what I'm perceived to be
REGULAR	you're playing at what you can't afford to be 'here' / 'here' / at home
NOVICE	I'm bein what I'm perceived to be 'there' / 'there' / on holiday / not my fault / what?
	What are you perceived as?
	What / see / what? So – cos you have more than me 'here'?
	So what?
	I got more'n they got / 'there'.
REGULAR	(*Dry*.) Make you feel important?

NOVICE	Makes me feel like you…
REGULAR	
NOVICE	
NOVICE	And ain't that what a holiday is for?
	For feelin better'n you did.
LOCAL	Betta than you are.
NOVICE	– I feel good about feelin good / *you* might be feelin bad but –
REGULAR	How is how I'm feeling any of your business?
	You know what? It is none of your business.
LOCAL	How you're feeling is –
REGULAR	nothing to do with *you*
LOCAL	how you're feelin is *his* business –
REGULAR	and *none* of yours.
LOCAL	
REGULAR	
REGULAR	Thank you.
	Beat.
NOVICE	Livin like this for the little weeks I can.
	…I like your life.
	Plastic fuckin fantastic fuckin –
REGULAR	it's not about –
NOVICE	pound to the dollar / dollar to the shekel / carryin the cash / su-fuckin-perb –
REGULAR	it's not all about –
NOVICE	money?
REGULAR	No.
NOVICE	No?

REGULAR	No.
LOCAL	No?
NOVICE	Heat, hotels and hard currency baby. Least I'm honest.

LOCAL *kisses her teeth*.

Andju can do your that as long as you want. Kiss your whatever as much as you want / yeh?

LOCAL *kisses her teeth*.

Carry on with your that –

LOCAL	I will.

LOCAL *kisses her teeth*.

NOVICE	Cos – he said… 'You're not like the local women.'

Beat

He said / 'You're not like the local women / you're *better*…' (*Baiting.*) Y'know.

(*As* BUMSTER.) '*Not beggin mi anytin and everythin every two minutes…*'

You know.

LOCAL *and* NOVICE *eyeball*.

(I) think I know what he means.

LOCAL	Yu n'noh nu'un 'bout what him (seh) –
NOVICE	don't I?
LOCAL	
NOVICE	
LOCAL	…Him said him want fe study / over inna your 'here'.

Beat.

LOCAL *watches* NOVICE.

Him seh…

'Mi gone go beach / gonna find myself a
somebody'

(*As* BUMSTER.) '*Noh matter which type a
what touriss / what piece a which kinda
touriss / mi a go beach an' find a piece a
that.*'

LOCAL *and* NOVICE *eyeball.*

Y'know.

'*Gonna find mi a som'ady / som'ady who
will get me to their "here" from my
"there" / I am / m'gonna – so mi cyan
study…*'

…He was top of his class…

You know.

NOVICE	So I fucked him / so what…
REGULAR	…I would've moved hotels anyway –

LOCAL *and* NOVICE

no you wouldn't.

REGULAR   I might have moved hotels (anyway) –

LOCAL *and* NOVICE

no you *wouldn't.*

REGULAR	…Honest.
LOCAL	Honest?
NOVICE	Honest?

Ere what.

At home / 'here' / a – he buys you a drink /
what? 'Honestly' – a – he buys you a drink
– a meal / so what? Suited and booted /
starters / the lot. He lyrics you / you giggle
/ you coy it / you laugh / you body
language you like him / you like him / you
leave / you fuck him / so what?

Honest.

LOCAL	The fool's fockin philosophy –
NOVICE	least *I'm* (honest) – you (*Re:* LOCAL.) say something?
LOCAL	Mi?
	No'un.
REGULAR	What I have / we / uh / is honest
LOCAL	no iss not –
REGULAR	I / uh / we –

LOCAL *and* NOVICE

	no iss not.
	Beat.
REGULAR	We had a good two weeks.
	We have a good two weeks.
NOVICE	You had a holiday –
REGULAR	I have a – friendship.
NOVICE	You just about have a fuckin friend –
REGULAR	I have a relationship
LOCAL	you're havin a fuckin laugh.
NOVICE	'Friends' don't rent recommended 'guesthouses'.
LOCAL	Not none that mi know.
	Friends don't leave for fifty weeks a year.
NOVICE	Not none that I know.
	Friends don't fuck…
	Well.
LOCAL	Friends don't fuck well / or friends don't fuck?
NOVICE	(*Amused.*) I like you.
LOCAL	(*Not amused.*) Mi n'like yu.
	Beat.

NOVICE	(*To* REGULAR.) And it ain't big. And it ain't clever / so you can cut your fuckin foul language right out –
REGULAR	I / we've been / I've been his 'friend' for years
LOCAL	…'years'?
REGULAR	I've been / I / uh / coming here for years

NOVICE *and* LOCAL

	'years'?
REGULAR	I've been / uh… coming to see / him / for years… I've been –
NOVICE	rentin-recommended-guesthouses / for years –
REGULAR	I've been coming / back / I come back / I've been back to –
NOVICE	see your fuckin 'friend'.
LOCAL	…For years…?
	Beat.
NOVICE	(*Dry.*) That what a 'friend' is for?
REGULAR	I've been back – I / uh / sending back –
NOVICE	what –
REGULAR	nothing
NOVICE	what?
REGULAR	*Nothing.*
LOCAL	Money…?
REGULAR	
LOCAL	
NOVICE	Shit.
REGULAR	…Because I (can) –
NOVICE	'Hard currency' is it? God, you this charitable at home?

REGULAR	It's not charity –
NOVICE	you this patronising at home? Pound to the dollar?
LOCAL	'Dollar to the shekel.'
NOVICE	(*To* LOCAL.) What do you think?
LOCAL	You still send him back hard currency / or yu did stop?
REGULAR	…You tell me.
	Beat.
LOCAL	(*Dry.*) Nice touch. Says a lot / says a lot aboutchu.
	Says a lot about your kind… ness.
REGULAR	You wouldn't know. You / uh / you don't know / you wouldn't / you wouldn't know / you both –
NOVICE	don't wanna (know) –
REGULAR	both of you / uh / you know / you just – don't –
LOCAL	want to –
REGULAR	know. You don't know.
	Beat.
NOVICE	You with who you would be / at home? You that?
	Know that.
	Know that much.
	(I) know I know thatchu're not that.
REGULAR	Are you the person 'there' that you are 'here' at home?
LOCAL	(*Re:* NOVICE.) Know she's not that.
NOVICE	You 'here'… strugglin to get a second look 'here' / you – who can't buy no attention 'here' / couldn't get it given to yer – 'here'

/ *you* – 'here' – ain't never asked yourself why you gettin what you getting 'there'?

Why you gettin what you get 'there' so... easy / so soon / so much –

REGULAR	what?
NOVICE	When so much a that so much / is so much above your station –
LOCAL	what?
NOVICE	(*Dry.*) Sorry to break it to ya – attention / so outta your league – so beyond whatchu coulda clocked – andju ain't never asked yourself why you getting what you got? 'There'?
LOCAL	Yu nevah ask yu'self –
NOVICE	that?
	See. Least me an' he is on the same sorta level –
LOCAL	no.
NOVICE	We the same / same sorta shit –
LOCAL	no.
NOVICE	Someone like him likin someone like you?
	Someone like him with someone like you?
	Know you need to ask yourself that / know you ain't asked yourself (that) –
REGULAR	and what have you –
NOVICE	– *how* you haven't / I don't (know) –
REGULAR	and what have you asked (yourself)?
NOVICE	She hasn't –
REGULAR	or don't you draw breath for long enough / your mouth doesn't stop for long enough for your ears to listen to anything anyone else might have to say?

NOVICE

              LOCAL *is amused.*

REGULAR   No. Yes. See.

REGULAR

NOVICE   If I was *you* – know I'd need to ask myself
              something – cos what kinda one-sided
              'friend' – sorry – '*relationship*' you got /
              got goin on?

              Beat.

              I'm *listenin.*

              Beat.

REGULAR   …There's a / we have a mutual –

NOVICE   whass he mutualise you back with?

LOCAL   Not y'wallet.

NOVICE   At your age – whass mutual about
              anything?

REGULAR   I don't need to explain anything about
              myself to you –

LOCAL   if yu shit worked you'd still be at home
              workin it.

              Wouldn'tcha?

REGULAR   Or you.

NOVICE   You got a fuck-buddy and you know it.

              Beat.

LOCAL   (If) your shit worked you wouldn't be
              travellin to my 'there' an' tryin to wo'k
              so'un where yu not wanted.

REGULAR   Oh I was wanted –

LOCAL   whatchu had was wanted – not whatchu is
              / truss mi –

REGULAR   how would you know?

LOCAL	If yu handled y'self right you'd still be at home rightin it – wu'dn'tcha? Truss mi.
NOVICE	Yeh she would
LOCAL	white woman over 'there' on her own at your age / say again what it was yu ha fi bring to the table…?
REGULAR	How would you know?
	Because… You seem to be the last to / to know / I don't mean to be… but you *do* seem to / to be the last / to know.
	About a lot of things.
	Beat.
	Don't you.
REGULAR	
LOCAL	
LOCAL	Is what yu tink him sees in yu?
REGULAR	
LOCAL	Is what it is yu tink *anybody* could see in yu?
REGULAR	
LOCAL	
LOCAL	*Really?*
REGULAR	
LOCAL	(*To* NOVICE.) And yu tink him see – *what?* – In yu?
NOVICE	
REGULAR	Keep telling yourself that. If you need to.
REGULAR	
LOCAL	
NOVICE	See. I had a thing / a me-and-he thing

REGULAR	a fucking-about thing
NOVICE	I bought the drinks
	I hired the rental
	He'd show me the sights / I'd take the view / so what
LOCAL	while he was taking time-outs with / her.
NOVICE	
LOCAL	That part a yu ting?
NOVICE	I didn't –
REGULAR	part of your 'so what' thing?
NOVICE	I didn't know about –
REGULAR	you're no different
NOVICE	I didn't know about you.
LOCAL	Didju know 'bout me?
NOVICE	Why would I ask?
REGULAR	You're no different –
NOVICE	to who?
LOCAL	To her.
REGULAR	I'm not like her / she's like them / those sand / beach / barely –
NOVICE	I'm not (like) –
REGULAR	barely clothed brazen things –
NOVICE	no! I'm *not* them
REGULAR	*I'm* not them.
NOVICE	You're a –
REGULAR	liar.
NOVICE	And you / we know it –
REGULAR	*liar.*
NOVICE	Liar? *Hypocrite*.
REGULAR	Hypocrite? – Prostitute

NOVICE	prostitute? – Whore.
REGULAR	Whore –
LOCAL	*tourist*.
	Beat.
NOVICE	How much respect he got for himself?
	How much respect you got for his self then?
	How much respect you got for *him*, Local?
	Shame.
	Beat.
	Where's your man?
	Where's your man at?
	Shame.
REGULAR	Where is he?
	Beat.
NOVICE	*That's* my answer.
REGULAR	Shame.
NOVICE	Right.
	Shame.
	Right shame.
	(*Baiting*.) You must be well proud / well prouda him.
REGULAR	(*Dry*.) You must be proud.
NOVICE	You must feel great.
REGULAR	(*Dry*.) You must feel *great*.
NOVICE	He must feel great / feel great about himself…
	Feel great about you / I bet.
REGULAR	I bet.
	(*As a* LOCAL MAN *looking* BUMSTER *up and down*.) '…*Koo-ya… Y'lookin sharp*.

Inna yu "fresh an' fancy" tings…

A joke mi ah joke.

How's Mummy / fambily?

Y'woman.

Beat.

Prouda their bwoy?

Know their bwoy…?

Know where their bwoy get him "fresh and fancy" tings from?

Nah. Mi nah tink so.

Shame.'

Beat.

LOCAL	Did he even tell you about me?
REGULAR	What is there to say about you?
	What do you have to say?
NOVICE	'Plaits for payment' / 'Canerow for cash'
REGULAR	that's you
NOVICE	'beauty on the beach' / 'shekels for a style'
REGULAR	that's you –

NOVICE *kisses her teeth badly trying to mock* LOCAL *as she had done it.*

that's you.

NOVICE	And by the way / you plait too tight.
LOCAL	Your scalp's too soft.
NOVICE	You're too rough.
LOCAL	And you're too easy.
NOVICE	
REGULAR	And why would I want to know about a woman that lets her man / fuck / other women… what would that make me? What does that make you?

LOCAL

REGULAR   What does that say about you?

LOCAL

NOVICE   I wouldn'ta said nuthin boutchu neither

LOCAL   you ask 'bout me?

REGULAR   I wouldn't have said anything if I was you.

NOVICE   I wouldn'ta said nuthin if I was you –

LOCAL   did yu ask over me

NOVICE   you don't come outta it lookin that lively do yer?

REGULAR   You don't come out of this looking that good.

LOCAL   …Did you ask…?

NOVICE   …I like your sign.

           Beat.

           (*Dry.*) I do like your sign.

           '*Local Styles at Local Prices.*'

           (*Dry.*) Lovely. Look what you got.

           Look what you got.

           …Lovely.

LOCAL   Mi? Mi nah work the beach –

NOVICE   (*Dry.*) hmm lovely –

LOCAL   don't have to work the beach –

REGULAR   (*Dry.*) lovely.

LOCAL   Don't have to tout for the trade. People see the sign / see *that* sign / an' people come to me now.

           People like… *you.*

NOVICE   (*Dry.*) Business is boomin.

LOCAL   No / business is *better.*

	'*It could suit –* '
REGULAR	(*As* AMERICAN TOURIST.) '*Y'know I don't know…*'
LOCAL	'*A change a style*'
REGULAR	(*As* AMERICAN TOURIST.) '*What did you say?*'
LOCAL	'*Live a likkle –* '
REGULAR	(*As* AMERICAN TOURIST.) '*I dunno –* '
LOCAL	'*y'noh it could –* '
REGULAR	(*As* AMERICAN TOURIST.) '*…Well…*'
LOCAL	'*Go on.*'
REGULAR	(*As* AMERICAN TOURIST.) '*Well – Y'know – like – could you – like / like… you could make me look like / like how – Bo Derek –* '
LOCAL	you saw the sign / saw the sign / that sign / you stopped / you did / you stepped up.
	Thass what I got.
NOVICE	(*Dry.*) That much.
LOCAL	More'n you got.
REGULAR	I don't think so. Dear.
LOCAL	And he paid.
	Him did pay.
REGULAR	
LOCAL	*He* did paid.
NOVICE	For what?
LOCAL	
NOVICE	…For what?
LOCAL	For the… '*Local Styles at Local Prices.*'
	For the sign… For the shelter. For me. Fe us.

REGULAR   He –

NOVICE   paid…

REGULAR

REGULAR

NOVICE   With what?

                Beat.

                Nervous now entcha.

                What's your sent-back-hard-earned hard
                currency been spent on…?

                I wonder.

LOCAL   I wouldn't be buyin a second and third
                drink of anythin for no man I don't know

NOVICE   I wouldn't fuck women off the beach I
                didn't know / but he did / does / with some
                old –

REGULAR   I'm not that old –

NOVICE   And where is he… where is he now?

LOCAL   Not 'here'.

                …Over your 'there'.

REGULAR

NOVICE   Obviously not with you

LOCAL   or you.

NOVICE   I wouldn't want him.

                So, what does that make you?

                NOVICE *is amused.*

                When did he last send some 'shekels' back
                / back to you?

LOCAL

NOVICE

NOVICE   (*To* LOCAL.) When did he last say he was
                coming back?

	Back to you?
	NOVICE *is amused*.
	I'm glad I ain't you.
REGULAR	(*Re:* LOCAL.) I'm glad I'm not you.
LOCAL	I wouldn't wanna be yous.
REGULAR	Shame.
LOCAL	Yu n'noh about shame an yu n'noh 'bout me / yu n'noh 'bout me an' he.
	…You wouldn't know 'bout them tings deyah…
	A big people ting.
	…You wouldn't know 'bout that…
	The me-an'-the-he is a long-term ting.
	This is a long-term ting / y'unnerstand?
	The we of it / is inna long (term) / lissen – me-an'-the-he of it is long-term tings / me and he been long-term from time / truss me.
	A trust ting.
	Truss mi.
REGULAR	Want to know about my trust?
NOVICE	No.
REGULAR	How much I trust?
LOCAL	No.
REGULAR	How much I trusted him?
NOVICE *and* LOCAL	
	No.
LOCAL	We… Wid no one else.
	Before we was –
NOVICE	what?
LOCAL	We never –

NOVICE	never did what?
LOCAL	Either a we / wid no one else…
NOVICE REGULAR	
LOCAL	I ask him.
	Yu noh.
	Y'unnerstan…
	Truss that.
	Truss mi.
	We truss that much…
	I ask him an' him prove – how much / how true / juss what –
REGULAR	what?
LOCAL	What kinda (truss) / we have.
	Truss mi.
	We never did / y'noh… bare-back / bare-back it / y'noh / flesh to flesh it / y'noh / wid nobody but we self / before.
	Beat.
	An' iss good.
	Feels… well – *feels* – y'nah?
	Yu n'noh.
	Yu n'noh 'bout them tings / a big people tings mi ah chat 'bout / a long-term ting mi a chat / a mi and he ting mi –
NOVICE	bare-back.
REGULAR	Bare-back?
NOVICE	I wouldn't bare-back with nobody, babe.
LOCAL	See.
NOVICE	'Trust me.' Don't trust nobody, babe.
LOCAL	See.

NOVICE	Not that much.
	Flesh to flesh? Forget that. Buy my own – bring my own – British Kitemark the works / mark my words –
LOCAL	thass yu.
NOVICE	That's me.
LOCAL	Young.
NOVICE	Young. That's me.
LOCAL	Yu mother teach yu that?
	Beat.
NOVICE	My mother taught me…
LOCAL	
NOVICE	
REGULAR	
NOVICE	
REGULAR	
NOVICE	What?
REGULAR	
NOVICE	What? What's the matter with (you) – nah –
REGULAR	
NOVICE	…Nah?
LOCAL	What?
REGULAR	
NOVICE	No you didn't…
LOCAL	
REGULAR	
REGULAR	…Do you want to know how much I trusted…?
LOCAL	
REGULAR	

LOCAL   …No…

                        Pause.

NOVICE   …*We* always / *I* always / we always *used* –

LOCAL *and* REGULAR
                        shut up.

                        Beat.

LOCAL   …You come 'there'.

                        …Invite yuself to my 'there'.

                        We ask yu / we trouble yu?

NOVICE   So what we can't go on holiday now?
                        Don't think so –

LOCAL   we never trouble yu / never asked yu –

NOVICE   that whatchu want? Can't go nowhere
                        without your say-so / don't think so / shit –
                        no one would be goin nowhere –

LOCAL   iss what kinda holiday yu lookin?

NOVICE   Thass our business.

LOCAL   You juss made it mine.

                        She juss made it mine.

                        Bare-back.

REGULAR

LOCAL

LOCAL   …Bess not be bringin your duttiness to my
                        door.

                        Beat.

REGULAR   Likewise.

LOCAL   *What?*

REGULAR

NOVICE   Ooh… Who is fuckin who?

REGULAR

LOCAL

NOVICE   And who's bein fucked (over) – ?

REGULAR   Will you just –

NOVICE   been fucked over

REGULAR   be quiet.

              Long pause.

LOCAL

REGULAR

NOVICE

LOCAL   Old…

NOVICE   you look

REGULAR   I am

LOCAL   she is

NOVICE   she's not that –

REGULAR   old.

              I am.

LOCAL   '*The Regular Tourist.*'

              The 'older white woman'.

              She been bein that.

REGULAR   I / I / I think to myself… people that are…
              are of… they're not gonna be young – very
              young / people.

              'Older.' Yes. I am. I feel… old.

LOCAL   '*The Novice.*'

NOVICE   Iss a holiday.

LOCAL   The Younger White Woman.

              '*The Younger White Woman.*'

              She been bein that.

NOVICE   *My* holiday.

REGULAR   She paid for it.

NOVICE   *Only* I paid for it.

                    So I can do what I want –

REGULAR   and did.

NOVICE   I didn't know about you.

REGULAR   How does it feel?

NOVICE *and* REGULAR
                    …'*The Local.*'

NOVICE, REGULAR *and* LOCAL
                    The Locals.

LOCAL   Me.

LOCAL 1   …Meh.

LOCAL 2   …Me.

LOCAL 1   Her.

LOCAL 2   Her.

LOCAL   Me – mi juss –

LOCAL 2   mi juss –

LOCAL 1   we juss –

LOCAL 2   'there'.

LOCAL   Local. All a we. All a we three.

LOCAL 1   *Local.*

LOCAL 2   Local to where them –

LOCAL   tek them holiday.

LOCAL 2   To where them –

LOCAL 1   haf their 'fun'.

LOCAL 2   To where them –

LOCAL 1   tek a break –

LOCAL   from who they is.

                    We 'local' to that. 'There.'

LOCAL 2   Me.

LOCAL 1   Meh.

LOCAL   Mi juss –

LOCAL 2   mi juss –

LOCAL 1   we juss live 'there'.

LOCAL   Local like that. 'There.'

LOCAL 2   'There' like that.

LOCAL   I just –

LOCAL 1   mi know –

LOCAL   I just live –

LOCAL 1 *and* LOCAL 2
                  we know

LOCAL   we just… live / live here.

LOCAL 2

LOCAL

LOCAL 1

                  End.

random

random was first performed at the Royal Court Theatre Downstairs, London, on 7 March 2008, performed by Nadine Marshall, and directed by Sacha Wares.

The play was revived and opened the Royal Court's Theatre Local season at the Elephant and Castle Shopping Centre on 3 March 2010, performed by Seroca Davis.

A filmed adaptation was broadcast on Channel 4 on 23 August 2011, with Nadine Marshall reprising her role from the original production, and directed by debbie tucker green.

286

Characters

SISTER
BROTHER
MUM
DAD
TEACHER
and others

One Black actress plays all characters.

Dialogue in ( ) is to be spoken.

Dialogue in [ ] is intention, not to be spoken.

Part Two is listed in the text; however, the play is to be performed straight through without any break.

PART ONE

SISTER   …And the su'un in the air –
in the room –
in the day –
like the
shadow of a shadow feelin…
off-key – I…
look the clock. Eyeball it.
It looks me back.
Stare the shit down –
it stares me right back.

Beat.

…Till it blinked first – loser.
Then changes its time… 7.37.
a.m.

So I –
give it my back –
roll on my front –
flex under the duvet
and lie there on the reluctant to get up –
a rubbish night's sleep
a restless night's sleep
for no reason at all.
Birds bitchin their birdsong outside.
People already on road.
Dogs in their yards barkin the shit outta
the neighbourhood.
This ent a morning to be peaceful
and the somethin in the air –
in the room –
in this day –
mekin mi shiver –

even tho my single duvet
is holdin on to me like my man –
who still don't phone –
should be.

Sun strugglin to be seen outside –
playin hide and seek with the clouds
like iss joke –
like iss shy –
losin its own game –
like we don't matter.
One a them, put that on – not that – not
that – *that* on – days a clothin confusion.
Truss mi.

BROTHER   7.38.
a.m.
Lay bad. Slept bad. Stretch (*Choops*.) –
don't help.
Birds sweetin their birdsong outside. Nice.
People already on road.

Neighbourhood Stafs barkin the shit outta
the area.
Sun doin what I do –
five more minutes –
ent ready for the up.
And the su'un in the air –
in the day –
in my room…

7.41.
a.m.

Iss now –
after the night –
iss now –
after all night –
iss only now – after night done and
daylight reach

that sleep comes to find me.
My turn.

SISTER	No worries 'bout rushin the bathroom –
	Mum done long time –
	Dad not doin day shifts –
	and that '*thing*' ent never up before me –
	step to his room – knock –
	don't lissen to hear nu'un –
	don't wanna hear nu'un –
	don't care –
	go in anyway.

'…You awake?'

Beat.

'You awake – '

BROTHER	this one can't be inna my dream.
SISTER	'You awake – '
BROTHER	nightmare.

BROTHER *kisses his teeth.*

SISTER	'I can borrow y'phone?'
BROTHER	'I'm sleepin.'
SISTER	'This room stinks – '
BROTHER	'come outta it then – '
SISTER	'so I can borrow y'phone – an' you ent sleepin – you sleepin? – how come yu sleepin all now? – mek mi borrow your phone – '
BROTHER	'you credit-less – your problem.'
SISTER	'Wanna use your sim in it – ennit – '
BROTHER	'find a next phone – or a next man yeh?'

Beat.

SISTER   '… I'ma 'llow that. Yeh?'

BROTHER *kisses his teeth.*

'Thass an answer? Thass your answer?'

BROTHER *kisses his teeth.*

BROTHER   'An' close back mi door.'

SISTER   Why he
think I wanna –
why he think I wanna be in his room that
[*s*]*tink.*
Why he think I wanna be –
in his room –
with him – that stinkin bwoy longer than
mi haf to – ask me.

8.13. Step downstairs.
Kitchen radio don't tune [in] right.
Little breakfast Mum mek, catch.
Juice finish.
Tea too hot.
Mum makin like it don't matter.

MUM   Porridge with black bits –
bu'n up bits in –
don't taste nice.
Iss her cookin that normally catch –
but…
something ketch me out today.
I see her watchin –
I stir it in
style it out
watch ar back –
till she turn and face she own bowl a
breakfas someting –
with ar smile –

and I eat my bowl a cornmeal
with its black bits in anyhow.

She don't want none.
She late down –
don't think I notice
that she nah mek the time fe a proper
'eat enough' –
a proper 'drink enough' –
of a morning.
She still tink bein young –
is bein invincible.
She still tink seh she young…
(*Amused*.) She like me.
She'll learn.
Like me.

An' she dress like iss summer
while spring still strugglin.
She see me lookin
and find su'un interestin
to face in ar bowl a cornflake.
She'll learn.

8.25.
'That whatchu wearin?'

SISTER	'Yeh.'
MUM	She wan' go up an' change.
	'You sure?'
SISTER	'Yeh.'
MUM	She not.
	'Y'warm enough?'
SISTER	'…Yeh.'
MUM	She won't be.
	'Y'sure?'

SISTER	'Mum.'
MUM	'Y'man ring yu?'
SISTER	'*Mum!*'
MUM	Thass all I said –
SISTER	So I... left – I leave – get my shit together an' gone. Not eaten enough – not drunk enough – (she don't need to know that) not time. I... step. To work. Open up and meet the day – and... ent nearly got enough clothes on neither. Iss cold. Truss mi. 8.32.
MUM	(*Amused.*) Now she garn. So I... dash mi dish a burn. But I – save enough in the pot f'him. Fe Junior. For when him come down. If him come down. ...Him should be down... MUM *listens*. MUM *shivers*.
SISTER	You spose to rule y'dog. Y'dog ent spose to rule yu. I see them Staf-Bull sportin youts

bein dragged by their beas's –
tryin an' stylin to look like they not.

8.45.
Everybody on the catch out
in the confusion a what to wear –
nobody gonna [ad]mit to bein wrong –
lookin wrong –
sweatin off –
or shiverin.

Them thass too hot
tryinta mask it lookin cool.
Them thass proper cold
stylin out they shivers –
big pops –
young she's –
young bucks
an' shorties.
Everybody ketch out
with this…
(*Gestures weather.*)

Beat.

9 o'clock.
I reach.
I…
nod my hellos –
smile…
cos I'm paid to.
Sit next to them
that I have to –
sippin my nasty cold cuppa work su'un –
to be sociable –
while I…
dream on the monthly cheque –
only thing thass keeping me here –
cos the Sallys –
the Johns –
the Deepaks –

the Janes –
the smalls talk –
the who did that –
the who saw that bein done –
the who did what last night – who woulda
done it better if it was them and who they
was diding it with –
truss mi…
None a that's keeping me here…

9.03.
Only.
I…
clock my off phone –
(if I can't phone my man on the 'find out'.
My man ent able to phone me on the
'excuse')
set my face
and start my work.

BROTHER	'Anythin to eat – '
MUM	Like iss hotel.
BROTHER	'Anythin to eat?'
MUM	Like mi favour landlady.
BROTHER	'What is there to – '
MUM	'Porridge.'
BROTHER	'That?'
MUM	'That.'
BROTHER	'That ent – '
MUM	'It is.'
BROTHER	'…Got black bits in.'
MUM	'Yu late down, porridge ha fe bu'n.' Heh.

Him watch the pot
watches me watchin
sights the juice – carton done
draws some milk –
only glasses it
cah him see me watchin.
Leaves out the empty glass
leaves out the still some in it milk
gives it the kiss on the side a *my* head
like I used to give it the kiss
on the side a *his*
when him was about ten…
Even then him would wipe it off –
with a smile –
thatchu couldn't.

I wipe his off
so him smile. He laugh – nearly –
as close as mi a go get from the big ting
that he is –
from the teenager he is –
but I'll tek it.

BROTHER   'She gone?'

MUM   'She gone.'

Him tek up him tings an' offs to school –
with a –

BROTHER   'Laters Mum.'

MUM   Like that'll do.
Him noh care that him n'eat enough –
nah do a proper 'drink enough' –
still tink bein young –
is bein… [invincible].
Ask mi –
how yu can mek a uniform look…
not like a uniform…
a tie look –
not like it spose to tie –

a trouser fit –
how you wannit to –
not how it meant to – *so low*?
A shirt flex, informal –
when it doin iss best to formalise?
A shoe look more like a sneak –
than a sneak look like a trainer?
A uniform look –
not how it intended –
but how yu intend?
…How them do that?

MUM *smiles*.

Heh.

BROTHER

She on a su'un of a mornin
if she down to bunnin porridge
yu haf'ee *try* to do that man –
that shit don't juss happen.
She think I ent eatin enough –
ent drinkin enough –
she gotta do betta than that black-up
pot of nastiness.

9.10.
Pass the Staf-Bull bredrins –

'Wha'gwa'an.'

Pass the youts doin the same as me –

'Move.'

They as late as me.

'Ennit tho.'

Pass thru the newsagent that doin
preschool breakfast business.

'Alright.'

Walkers Ready Salted fill the gap.
Coke's finest juicin the cracks.
Girls bein loud –
bredrins bein louder –

'Yeh – yu nice – you – not y'frien' – *you*'

sight my mans them –

'Bless.'

An' step to the schoolhouse
phonin the sour-face sis –
that I got
who still screwin 'bout my mobile –
that I got
holdin a grudge –
how she do
feel to show her a little love –
how iss done
but her phone's lock off...
So leave her a stink message instead.

MUM   I...
               flick on the Phillip and the Holly –
               'pon the kitchen TV set
               look to the places and spaces
               where my big two babies were
               and set to clearing and cleanin what's left
               behind.
               Like I'm their keeper –
               their cleaner –
               their... heh
               their mum.

               And as her cornflake bowl
               is scrape free of wet leftovers
               and the dregs of the drinks
               is sunk inna the sink
               and the crumbs and the marks and milk

and signs of their mess
is wiped away...
The sun breaks out
and decides it's gonna show.
'My days.'

Holly and Phil still a chat them shit
still deep inna it –
the clean-up kitchen
waits for the next time –
the washin-up drips to it's dry –
the sun shoots a shine thru the window –
I watch it –
I...
see it.
But –
nah feel it.
Cah... still I ketch a –
shiver of the shadow of the shadow of the
day.

SISTER   How these people come to work?
How these people come to work –
but don't wanna work?
Ask me?!
If you don't wanna work –
don't come –
nah –
if you come –
don't reach cos your only reason is
to come by *me* and chat *your* shit
inna *my* ears
'bout how much you hate it.
I hate it.
Hate them.
Hate hearin –
Sally's
John's
Deepak's

and Jane's
business.
Hate havin to hear it – day in day out –
why they think I wanna hear that?
Why they think I care – and if Sally flicks
that hair of *hers*
near *my* face –
again…
truss –
mi.
[They] chat their shit to me –
[they] sit back
they chattin their shit to me
spectin me to –
chat shit back to them –
spectin me to –
chat *my* shit back to them
I got friends f'that –
I got –
fambily f'that –
truss mi –
I got me a *man* fe that…
Well.
Sort of.

BROTHER Little bit late better'n not at all.
Little bit late better than not [at all] – yeh?
Soon come betta than don't come – y'get –
sometime betta than never –
can't tell me it ent –
rock up an' reach a little ten minutes down
– yeh?

TEACHER 'Twenty'

BROTHER she says. But I'm there.

TEACHER 'Not good enough – '

BROTHER she says – but I reach.

TEACHER	'Just.'
BROTHER	She says. Givin me grief when there's others – truss [mi] *others* – on the in behind me – y'get? – diggin their Walkers breakfast out their teet still. Now. I ain't that – I ent that bad blastin me out – an' tellin me iss for my own good – when there's others worss! Blatant. (*Dry*.) 'Know yu miss me Miss'
TEACHER	'Siddown'
BROTHER	's'only juss a ten – '
TEACHER	'twenty – '
BROTHER	'I can't help it if you missin me after – '
TEACHER	'Sit. Down.'
BROTHER	' – after a ten minutes – '
TEACHER	'*twenty*.'
	Beat.
BROTHER	See. I give ar joke even when she try all her – hardness and teacherness – an' teacher-trainin tactics – we still gotta little –
TEACHER	'SIT. DOWN!'
BROTHER	She say I got potential – I *know* I got potential –

but come on now
bare blastin me out in fronta my…
when I was only ten –

TEACHER   '*twenty*'

BROTHER   late. Come on now…
Don't mek mi have to say somethin.

SISTER   Sally… told John
some su'un 'bout Deepak…
that Deepak never want John to know
and never know Sally
was tellin him.
Jane see it all –
and ent sayin shit –
Deepak vex –
John actin ignorant –
Sally sayin she sorry –
twistin her hair ends with the stress ar
mout' put her in – 'bout askin me:
What do I think?

SISTER *kisses her teeth.*

MUM   'Wha' yu want fe dinner?'

Beat.

'Is whatchu want fe yu dinner?'

Beat.

Him still asleep –
so him a go get what him given.
Heh.
So mi look to put mi su'un on
to meet an' greet the outside worl' in –
but iss…
One a them – put that – not that – *that* on
weather days a clothin confusion

cah the sun still nah lookin like iss sure.
Hmm.
So mi dress –
mi check –
mi re-dress again an' –

DAD   Lamb.

MUM   Hmm?

DAD   Lamb.

MUM   Hmph.
               The dead awake.

SISTER   Dad the kinda dad who…
               don't say much.
               Unless he have to.
               Who…
               don't say nuthin –
               unless he want to –
               who –
               won't say anythin
               unless he feel to –
               a –
               'Wha' yu want?
               Wha' yu seh?
               Wha' yu do?
               Where yu deyah?'
               Usually goddit covered, y'get.

               He the kinda dad who a –
               'hmm'
               can make you smile.
               A silence…
               can make you look
               a pause
               can make you confess
               truss mi –
               a eyebrow
               can make you nervous.

He the kinda dad who kinda…
he kinda…
kind.

Deepak lunchin on his own –
wanna know if I wanna join him.
Sally still lookin sorrowful –
sippin on her SlimFast *fast*
her hair juss lookin –
a mess a stress now –
Jane chattin shit –
nervous 'bout who to ally herself wid –
tho nobody don't really want her –
and John chicken out
and gone for the takeout –
Me?
I lie.
Say I wanna work thru lunch…
On my ownsome.

Morning done.
At last.

1 o'clock.

MUM   Why yu can't walk inna ones and twos?
               That gone outta fashion?
               'Pon street – why yu can't walk inna –
               yu noh haf fe bunch up
               crowd up
               loaft street
               inna – posse
               crew
               pack
               or whatever dem wan' call it.
               Why dem cyan' walk inna ones and twos?

               Whole heap a people 'pon pavement –
               whole heap a youts 'pon road.
               How can a somebody know so much
               people-dem –

them all know each other?
Them nah noh each other –
all in them bastardise version
a them same uniform.
The same kinda different
got them lookin –
all the same
an'
tryin too hard – to look hard.

Eatin out on street
for the worl' to see
like them never nyam before –
like them noh raise –
like them noh raised at all –
like them nevah have no Mooma an'
no Poopa
to manners their manners.

Half a them nah dress right neither –
too cold –
mi see it.
Too hot –
mi see it.
Not enough clothes on –
not long enough clothes on –
gyal dem got more mout' than the boys…
heh
kinda remind me of –
me.

Cross the road
and look the white man butchers
where mi a go get mi meat from.
Lamb.

Fe him at home.

1.27.

SISTER   If I was a man –
                    nah – but *wait* –
                    if I was *my* man
                    truss it –
                    thass *right* –
                    I woulda been phonin *me* quick time
                    from time
                    for the longest time… right.

                    Even tho my mobile been on lock down
                    that don't matter –
                    that can't distract –
                    nu'un to stop him
                    flexin a text –
                    voicemailin me a little 'sorry' –
                    tryin a ting
                    try a ting –
                    try anything.
                    Just…
                    try man.

                    2.10.

DAD   'Smoddy phone.'

MUM   Thass my welcome back.

DAD   'Smoddy phone.'

MUM   My welcome home.

                    'Who?'

DAD   'Mi nah noh.'

                    Beat.

MUM   'Y'pick up?'

DAD   'Sleepin.'

MUM   'Butchu hear it.'

DAD   'Hmmph.'

MUM	'Butchu nah pick it up?'
DAD	'Woulda one a your people dem – '
MUM	'How yu know?'
DAD	'Mi noh.'
MUM	So him psychic now.
	We inna psychic someting –
	evidently –
	but mi never noh –
	nevah realise me husband secret talent.
	Over all these long years.
	H'evidently.
	My husban' one a dem man who…
	don't say much –
	unless him haf to –
	who don't say nuthin –
	unless him want to…
	Who nah pick up the phone –
	cah him *psychic* to raas –
	'We got lamb chops.'
DAD	'We got company.'
MUM	'Huh?'
DAD	'We got a smoddy at the door.'
MUM	I –
	turn.
	Mi
	look.
	He, right –
	the shadow of some somebodies –
	standin there –
	for me to open.
	I
	see them –
	them
	see me –

them nod a uniformed, trained politeness
I look back – see me husband
strainin to see…

Him never psychic this one.

Beat.

[Iss the] Police.

SISTER 'Come home.'
What I thought was from my man
is from my mum.
'Come home. Now.'
One message from her.
And one *stink* message from Junior
from morning.
He think he's funny – carry on
thinks he's comedian – carry on
as my finger runs to find delete.
Now *thass* funny bruv.

'Come home. Now.'

Beat.

Deepak looks over –
knows not to ask –
he still in his own misery anyhow.
John concentrating on his eat out –
Jane only one to say –
'Where you goin?'
'…Home.'
Sally ears prick –
flicks her bottle-blonde shit –
gets the strength to speak in her disgrace –
'You sick?'
'…I'm sick.' (Of you.)
Sally on the –
'Aaah. You alright?'
Deepak attack now with the –

'How can she be alright – when she says
she's sick?'
Sally siddown sharp
pullin on her hair a mess.
John heads up with a –
'We'll let them know –
anything you want covered?'
Fe them to frigg up my work.
Hell no.
Log off – password padlock – quick-time.
'Hope you feel better'
then he's back to his burger –
they back to their work –
the air of the office politics
back to what it was.
I…
Leave.
2.13.

MUM   'Bout –
                     can they come in?

                     They still there
                     lookin at me
                     lookin at them
                     they lookin past me at him
                     'bout…
                     'Can they come in?'
                     Two a them Police cars
                     park outside
                     our yard.
                     Right outside
                     our yard.
                     …And all a my
                     whys?
                     All a my
                     who's
                     all a my
                     where's

all a my
what's
and whens and whyfors
rampaging all thru my –
mind
only come out as a quiet

…No.

Look back to my husband
who looks forward – at them.
We united on this one.

'Don't be bringin no Polices to my door.'
That was his first law.
'And if they come –
an' one a yous kids in trouble if they do –
don't let even a one a them in'
that was his second.
And the kids would eyes to the sky and
sigh
and
'no Dad'
and
'yes Dad'
and
bored a the lecture before it begin.
'Never trouble trouble till trouble trouble
yu.'
That was mine.
Maybe this someone else's trouble.
'Bout.
'Can we come in.'
The law still outside
standin on our doorstep
waitin on a answer…

'No.'

Beat.

Beat.

Dark boots an' heavy shoes
inna my house.

On my carpet.

Dark boots
an' heavy shoes –
on my clean carpet
in my good room –
in my front room –
my visitor room –
my room fe best –
fe formal –
not even fe fambily.
Dark boots and heavy shoes –
beatin down my
for best carpet
without a second thought…
from them.
Outside shoes ent worn in this house –
an'
'no I don't wan' no cup a tea.'
An'
ennit for me to offer?
an'
'Yes, I am his wife –
his mother –
they my kids –
he my Son.'
And –

DAD   'Yes – I am ar husban'
their father –
an' no – mi nah want no cup a tea –
thass fe us to offer –
an' no
mi noh wan' fe sit. Neither.'

SISTER   If Mum took sick
                Dad should be lookin after her.

                Dad would ring.
                Wouldn't stop ringin.

                If Dad took sick
                Mum would manage.
                Always has.

                Text her I'm comin –
                phone Junior to see if he know more'n I do
                but he doin what I do
                thinkin he smart –
                locked off his phone.

                Leave him a stink message instead.

                MUM *is bewildered.*

MUM   Him tink seh me sittin
                is some kinda betrayal.
                Can see it
                how he look 'pon me – a flicker as me do
                it
                behind he's eyes.
                I catch it
                an' dash it
                cah mi ha'fe siddown
                before mi drop down.

                '…Mi dawta… Mi dawta.
                Mek mi phone mi dawta.
                I want to phone mi [*dawta*] – I have to
                phone our – tell them we wan' phone our
                [dawta] – I want her here – I want her
                here.'

                Beat.

                '…How yu know iss him?'

Beat.

'How yu know – ?'

Them a chat 'bout
'eyewitness'
an'
'description'
an'
'ID' him a carry –
an'
seems that –
they gotta view
of my Son
of
who my Son is –
where my Son is
of
who them tink seh my Son is
and doin what.
…1.30 – they say. Lunch break.
About – 1.30 – on the high street.
Near by the butchers.
A 'altercation'
a – 'attack' –
a – 'yout – another yout' –
they think.
'Random.'
Them a chat 'bout…
su'un su'un
them mout' move –
but me ear them juss…
rebel…
an'
refuse…
an'
try an' stop hear.

Beat.

I want mi dawta. Here.
Them –
offer them mobile
but
I look fe mi landline
can't dial –
husband do –
he can't say…
I do – only…
'Come home.
Come home now.'

2.07.
Say nu'un else.

Look to my husband
who stays standin.
All eyes on them
them who look more awkward than we do.
I –
shiver –
he –
offer them tea
they too keen in their trained acceptance
that breaks the silence
textbook
how it should.

He stands
good an' straight
my man.

Like the good straight man him is
like the good straight man mi marry
asks them them sugar preference
then tells them… straight:

'I don't believe you.'

SISTER   Dad always said
                'Don't bring no Polices back –

don't let no Polices in'
same thing he'd say 'bout white people –
Mum'd chip in with some
old-skool su'un 'bout –
trouble an' trouble – reh teh teh
but we never lissen good
we be bored by that bit –
truss mi.

So it odd.

Seein –
not a one
but a two piece a Police cars
outside our yard.
For all to see.
Obvious.
For all to know.
Blatant.
For all to chat 'bout.
Shame.

Mum gonna cuss.
Dad gonna be pissed.
They ent here for me –
so
it ent my arse
thass gonna get kicked –
Junior –
better have one piece a excuse.

MUM   I see that the too-sweet tea
             don't sweet them.

             See he sweet it too much.
             On purpose.
             How he do –
             with people he don't like.
             Them nah sey nu'un
             'bout his lack of belief.

Them nah sey nu'un
'bout his nasty tea
too trained in a unnatural politeness
to let their guard…
slip.
They watch us.
We watch them.
As they sit sat
sip
swallow
and tink what part of they script
they gonna select next.

SISTER …Reh.
Shoes on in the front room.
They better be Police.
Boots on in the front room.

They better be brave dred.

Smell Dad's too-sweet tea a mile off
muss be poisonin them
with sugar.
Mum sat –
lookin shook.
Dad standin
lookin like he have to.
Su'un too quiet 'bout the house
su'un not right.
Step in – sock-foot
and see the two uniforms
and a plain clothes
sippin their too-sweet somethin.

MUM 'This our dawta.'

SISTER Says Mum.
I don't bother to 'hi' a hello.
2.53.

MUM

I… uh…
Look to mi husban'
hold on to mi gurl.
She do what I do
if sense never leave me –
she look them up an' down –
sights them outside shoes inside
an' she ask an' she ask an' she h'ask an' –

SISTER

'How yu know iss him – how yu know he
was there – how yu know iss not
somebody who favour? How y'know he
ent on road – ent at he's girls – one a he's
girls – how yu don't know that? How
y'know he ent juss late? How y'know he
ent with he's spars –
Spars?
Friends – man-dem – mates – bredrins –
no…
not a 'gang'.
Why you here?
Why you sittin here?
Why you in here sittin on *my* mum's good
sofa –
in *your* outside shoes –
drinking *my* dad's sweet tea –
an' askin 'bout my *brother* –
why you here? Why you – why you *here*?'

Beat.

Beat.

So they bring out their…
clear plastic bag
of a conversation stopper.
So all can –
clearly see
what they –
clearly
tryinta say.

Mum looks –
looks away.
Dad lookin at them
still.
I clock the bag
and its content
and –
deny.

'So it look like he's phone – what?
Nuff mans carry dem same piece a su'un.
So it look like he's phone – *what*?
My number last dial on it – so?
So it look like he's phone – *yeh* – that is
my number – yeh – that is his phone then.
So? And? *What?*…'

'…What's with the brown on it?'
Oh.
Blood.

…Since when does a mans bleed brown?

…When the blood is old and dry.

Oh.

Beat.

Why ent we…
where he is?

'…Why ent we –
where he is –
why ent we gone?

Why ent we in one a your
flash pig cars
with your sirens on?
What if he's shook?

What if he's not sure –
and what the fuck you think he's family's
for?'

What if he's callin –

for his dad –
his mum –
…Me?

Beat.

…And they sip their tea –
and they sat there sittin –
tryin to
pacify our worry
with a…

'There's no need to hurry,
there's no need to hurry.

There is no

need
to
hurry.'

…We already way too late.
…And never even know it.

PART TWO

SISTER   Dad went down to ID my brother.
                     I went down to support our dad.

                     Dad went in
                     I didn't have to follow.
                     But...

                     Brother had a –
                     birthmark.
                     Here.
                     Juss like me.
                     But his been
                     cut thru
                     with a chunk of him gone
                     now.
                     He had an eye
                     two.
                     Now he got juss one.
                     They try to pretty it up
                     mek it look like he winkin...
                     But
                     ...you can't pretty up
                     whass horrific.
                     Y'not meant to.

                     His mout'
                     look like a clown –
                     now
                     wider than it should be.
                     It slashed so much on a one side
                     from there
                     to there.

                     That juss he's face.
                     Thass juss the ones that would mark him,
                     wouldn't kill him.

Apparently.

Thass juss the ones he'd haveta live with.
Have had to live with.

He have plenty little
like – uh – like –
(*Gestures forearms.*)
look like he a self-harmer
but proof he fought back.
Then they have to turn him
and
hold him
an'
lie him on his side
an'
so we could see – could see good
lookin hard to see.

Point of entry.
The killer cut.

You have to look hard
to look hard.

This was…
the smallest.
The cleanest.
The easiest to miss
part of it all.
Truss mi.
Juss –
round.
(*Gestures.*)
From the back –
those rules is broken then –
thru to –
(*Gestures.*)
punctured his…
su'un – important.
But.

Not no gash.
Not no not sure.
Not no random.
Juss a small
deep
sorta
round
sorta
hole.
In him.

Easy to miss.
Easy to miss.

Easy to miss.

Beat.

And our dad the kinda dad who…
Who…
don't say nuthin –
unless he –
who won't say anythin –
unless…
Dad tryin to say somethin.
Dad's tryin to say somethin
but
…nu'un won't [come out]…

I watch.
Watch him.
…He's embarrassed.
I watch his embarrassment.
I can't look away.

They lift us back
in a unmarked ride,
tho I can still tell iss one of theirs.
And me an' Dad sit
in the back –
like kids

as they drive us home
havin to ask directions.
The only thing breakin the heavy silence.

And I still ent stopped
starin at Dad.
Dad still ent stopped
lookin away
and we pass the everyday
the life-goes-on
the
people goin-about-they-business
the
people who don't know – won't know –
don't got no idea.

We pass the spot.
I ask –
to stop. Get let out and get out.
As they drive on.

Standin by the yellow an' blue murder
board
the battlefield where brother slain.
Alone.
Me on my own.
'Cept for the boys in blue
guarding the pavement piece
I guess.
Watchin
the Police tape bouncing
in the breeze.
Too late.

Passerby passes by
don't look once
let alone twice
used to it.

Some too-old young men
in low-bats an' hoodies
holdin bunches of

proper flowers
not no garage shit
sight me
and say:
'...Sorry sis.
He was safe.'

Like I don't know.

Baby women
barely breakin their teens
upset
see me
upset
ask brazen as brazen baby women do
'Is it true he was your brother?'

Beat.

'Nah man – wrong'
she say
'if it was some skank little hoodrat then – '

That would be alright?

'He was nice'
she say
'[he] said I was ['nice'] – usedta clock him
inna mornins outside the Asian man
shop...
Coke an' crisp... '
She looks to the spot
starts singin some r'n'b tune
some dry r'n'b tune
as a gesture
dry lyrics
as a tribute.
Shit voice.
Shit song.
If she proper knew him
she woulda know
he was a bashment man.

A…
street shrine starts to stack up
flowers
candles
cards
T-shirts
tags
teddy bears
Coke an' crisp
the flag of our island
Garvey's colours of Africa –
a note from his form teacher
signed with a smile…
Shrine really start to pack up.

A baby mother puts down her contribution
steps back admires
nods me
knows me
her baby sleeps on
'Gonna mek it betta than
them mans dem
down them other ends'
she sey.
'This a proper shrine.
Bless.'
And she gone.
A sea –
of he's schoolpeeps
stand there.
Nuff.
In a heavy silence.
With their –
headphones long off
their
mobile phones
on silent
their schoolbags still slung
on their

uniformed backs.
The homegurls heng on to each other –
homeboys
hold each other up
as they silently shake
shook.
Hidin their faces
in each other's shoulders
witnessin somethin they shouldn't
and…
cry.

The press
pressin
the picturesque for a bite.
Their – blue-eyed reporters
shieldin their zeal
for a – 'good', 'urban' story
stepping into these sides
askin foolish questions
soundbitin so-called 'solutions'
in seconds.
Feelin brave askin a hard-lookin 'hoodie'
what he think.
Only to find
under the cloak of Adidas
is a brotha
whose eyes don't stop flowin.
Wet raw
with weepin.
But…
they don't show that bit tho.

Death usedta be for the old.

An' still the street shrine
propah packs up
stacks up
with Black on Black love.
Mum won't go.

	Point-blank
	won't go.
MUM	So they can look
	and call me 'dignified'
	look
	and call me 'strong'
	look
	and see *me* cryin
	look
	glad it not them
	look
	and wonder where the smoke was
	cos *su'un* muss have force the fire.
	(*Dry.*) Right?
	I don't got nuthin nice to say.
	Nu'un polite
	nu'un
	broadcastable
	nu'un
	righteous
	nu'un forgivin
	juss pure…
SISTER	She don't say.
	Mum won't go.
	Point-blank.
	She sittin as she was
	as she has been
	in her same spot in the front room
	with some – Victim Support su'un su'un
	sat by her now
	who got it right.
	With their shoes off.
	But
	makin no difference
	to the difference we now got.
	Can't make this difference
	go away.

Dad – Dad's
takin the phone calls.
Bewildered by it.
Family doin family things
phonin
findin out
somebody gotta say
somebody gotta tellem.
Dad doin a –
bad
job of it
but…
Mum don't want no one round the house.
Not no one.

Sally, John, Deepak an' Jane
rock up on the doorstep.
Unannounced
unasked
uneasy.
Jane hidin behind John
Sally's eye wet,
Deepak bein brave
steps up an' says
'They've heard.
And they just wanted to say –
if there's anything
at any time
any a them
can do…'

Why Jane's playin shy I don't know
and who ask Sally fe bawl
she never know my brother
she don't even know me
and I look them
and I watch them
an' I see their unease
an' I say
'Iss alright.'

John not buyin it
says in a second
'Nah iss not.
We juss wanted you to know. Y'know?'
Which was… [nice]

They don't ask to come in.
They don't overstay.
Gimme a touch as they go –
John the only one to look back
seein me seein them leave.
And nods.
And leaves me watchin.

Beat.

Beat.

I lissen

and I hear…

Silence.

I hear – an' juss get –

Silence.

Whole heap a witness
Polices say.
Whole heap a somebodies
on street.
Saw.
Whole heap a peeps
on road
was present.
But I lissen –
hard –
an' still I hear…

Silence.

Silence shoutin the loudest.
Cos it seem that
now no one wanna witness
what happened

to my Brother.

Mum wants to see his body.
Dad tell ar she don't.
Mum wants to see his body.
Dad tells her, 'Don't.'
Mum tells me

MUM   'I-wants-to-see-my-Son's-body.'

SISTER   I tell her –
               'She won't.'
               She looks on me and Dad
               like
               we the perpetrators now
               cuts her eye and asks

MUM   'You sure it was him?'

SISTER   'Yeh. It was.'

MUM   'How yu know?'

SISTER   Dad says, 'It was.'

MUM   'Y'see his mark?'

SISTER   I say… Yeh.

MUM   'Yu see his mark?'

SISTER   Dad says, 'Yeh' too.

MUM   'Y'sure it was him?'

SISTER   'Yeh. It was him, Mum.'

MUM   'Y'sure it was *him*?'

SISTER   Dad nods.

	Mum not missin a beat:
MUM	'Y'sure he was dead?'
SISTER	Support Officer says somethin quietly in Mum's ear. Mum stays eyes on me throwing out her bad looks.
MUM	'Y'sure he was *dead*?'
SISTER	Support Officer keeps sayin her su'un hard in Mum's ear gives Mum a touch keeps talking till Mum kisses her teeth at me looks away from me looks to the Support Officer and gives *her* a nod. What did I do? *Beat.* Dad's done took the phone off its hook and left it there. Hanging. I'm told not to touch it – not to hook it back – not to phone out – not to answer it – not to go near it – Dad's had enough 'but – ' he don't wanna hear 'but – ' don't wanna hear me

'but – '
don't wanna hear what I got to say
…Dad's had enough.
But…

Su'un in the kitchen
startin to smell tho.
Mum don't care.
Dad don't wanna know.
But somethin in the kitchen
is startin to [stink] –
Dad don't want me in there –
'but – '
Dad don't want me – in there
'but – '
Dad – don't want me.

As he sits in the stink
comin from the bag
from the white man butchers
sittin on the side goin wrenk.

Beat.

My room ent holdin nuthin for me.
My room ent holdin [nuthin for me] –
it ent holdin nuthin for me now.
Left as I left it
this morning
when he was still asleep
in his room
this morning
when he was still –
in his room…
this morning.

So I go in he's.
He would kill me if he knew.

And it still stinks.

Of the sleep
of the sweat-off

of the young man
of… my brother.
I close back the door
to keep it in.
Sit on the floor –
finding a clean bit –

back to the wall and
wait…

It don't smell sweeter
like I tho't it would.
Still stinks as it did.
As bad as it did
and his bed's
as unmade as it was
and he's garms is
still spread all over
and he's computer's still on standby
cos he didn't give a fuck about goin green
and he's books is unread
and he's mags ent as outta sight as he tho't
and he's weights
lie waitin
and he's too-strong-young-buck aftershave
lies open-top
and he's hair sheen…

stands alone
waitin on the shaved head
to come back.

And his poster of Danai
hangs over his bed
both of us clockin
it's as empty as it will be
now.
So I take a deep –
(*Inhales.*)
and don't wanna lose the strength

of his bedroom su'un.
Ever.

And the house is quiet...
y'know?
The house that never was...
is well quiet.

And I open his top drawer
boxers and socks
close it in case he know.
Open his second drawer –
tops an' tees
draw open his third...
sweat-tops sweatpants –
close it carefully.
...Juss in case he's watchin.

Beat.

Birds is silent
grievin as well.
Neighbourhood Stafs still
barkin the shit outta the area –
an' the sun –
the sun decided it's done for the day –
and this room...
(*Inhales deeply.*)

Close back his
drawer
close back his
door –
keep his stink in.
Step down the – too-quiet stairs
past the stank Dad still sittin in
from the kitchen.
Pass the socked Support Officer
struggling –
in the best room
with our...

my

destroyed mum.
And I…
step out.

Right.
Right.

End.

www.nickhernbooks.co.uk

facebook.com/nickhernbooks

twitter.com/nickhernbooks